# *Weekend Driver*
# **San Diego**

# *Weekend Driver*
# San Diego

### Jack Brandais

## Sunbelt Publications
### San Diego, California

*Weekend Driver San Diego*
Sunbelt Publications, Inc.
Copyright ©2004 Jack Brandais
All rights reserved. First edition 2004. Second printing 2004

Edited by Jennifer Redmond
Photos and book design by Jack Brandais, www.weekenddriver.com
Base maps courtesy of SANGIS. Used with permission. www.sangis.org
Project management by Jennifer Redmond
Printed in the United States of America

Sunbelt Publications, Inc.
P.O. Box 191126
San Diego, CA 92159-1126
(619) 258-4911, fax: (619) 258-4916
www.sunbeltbooks.com

"Adventures in the Natural History and Cultural Heritage of the Californias"
A Series Edited by Lowell Lindsay

07  06  05  04        5  4  3  2

Library of Congress Cataloging-in-Publication Data

Brandais, Jack, 1958-

Weekend Driver : San Diego : Day drives in and around San Diego / Jack Brandais. — 1st ed.
    p. cm. — (Adventures in cultural and natural history)
Includes bibliographical references and index.
ISBN 0-932653-63-4
1.  San Diego Region (Calif.) — Tours. 2.  Automobile travel — California — San Diego Region
— Guidebooks. I. Title. II. Series.

F869.S22 .B72 2004
917.94'98504–dc22

                                        2003019928

Cover design by Handmade Graphics and Computer Concepts.

Cover background map Copyright ©2002 Automobile Club of Southern California. All rights
reserved. Reproduced by permission.

Photo of Jack Brandais by Greg Lambert

# *Weekend Driver*
# San Diego

## *Introduction*

# Get Out Of Town

### *Fill Up the Tank and Head to the Hills*

**I**n San Diego and Southern California, where the car is king, it's always surprising how many people have never gotten off the freeway, never took that "other turn," never explored strange, new roads.

This is such a beautiful part of the country, it's almost a shame most of the residents never venture from the three-bedroom-ranch on some street with a phony Spanish name.

Of course, if they did, the sometimes wide-open roads and unspoiled vistas in this book wouldn't be so wide-open and

At the time of this book's printing, the fires of 2003 were just subsiding, with an untold amount of damage to San Diego's backcountry. Use good judgement in traversing roads in fire-damaged areas, call ahead for site and road info when in doubt, and please practice good fire safety.

**Loveland Reservoir in the spring.**

unspoiled.

So let's keep this our little secret.

Don't tell anyone about the spots in the mountains where views go all the way to the ocean.

Keep secret the near-empty beaches and places where RVs can hook up for just a few dollars a night.

And certainly don't blab about the fantastic twisting roads for sports cars or dirt roads for SUVs.

**T**he genesis for this book came when I was a kid. On Sundays, my folks would load us into our 1956 Chevy (or later the 1964 Pontiac) for rides in the country. Oh, and we'd stop by the spot in Escondido that had a "gas war" — four corners of gas stations that actually competed on prices.

We'd go to places like Rancho Santa Fe, slowing down to about 15 miles an hour so my dad and mom could see the big houses — just imagine how that embarrassed a 10-year-old. Or up to Cuyamaca Rancho State Park for a picnic or a hike.

## Route-O-Matic Symbols

### Family Stuff

**Stuff For Kids:** Look for good things to see and fun stuff to do.

**Not For Kids:** Leave them at home. Might have casinos or just might be boring for tots but fun and/or romantic for adults.

### Route Type

**A Must For Locals:** If you consider yourself a local, you need to know this route.

**Rubbernecker Special:** This is a drive my dad would have loved... lots of stuff to see at 15 miles per hour.

**Backyard Byway:** A surprising route that's very close to the urban area.

**Horse Friendly:** There are a lot of places to take horses; a couple of our routes are especially for drivers *and* equines.

**Nature Lovers Ride:** Spectacular scenery and places to picnic, hike, and park dominate these routes.

## More Route-O-Matic Symbols

### On The Road

Good route for sports cars, with twists and mostly good pavement. Might also include an optional dirt stretch that doesn't necessarily require an SUV.

Motorcycle tourers would have a great time. No dirt to mess up those chrome heads.

The drive includes dirt roads... a chance to utilize that high clearance and, if you have it, all-wheel-drive or four-wheel-drive.

### For More Information

Sections include Web sites, phone numbers, and other information on the attractions mentioned in each chapter.

### Maps And Directions

- Due to publishing limits and the size of the maps, all the street names aren't there. Be sure to follow the directions... or just get lost and enjoy exploring the unknown.

A day drive then, and now, is an inexpensive way to take a quick vacation.

In June 2000, the "Weekend Driver" column first appeared in the "Wheels" section of the *San Diego Union-Tribune*. At last, I could take drives and share my experiences with others.

Over the years, I've received e-mails and letters from driving enthusiasts, suggesting routes and asking me to leave a few secrets. Some secrets are still secure, but I couldn't leave everything out.

More recently, I've been writing the "Tank of Gas" features for the *Union-Tribune*'s "Night and Day" section.

This book is a compilation and update of the original "Weekend Driver" columns, information from "Tank of Gas," plus several drives exclusive to the book. If you take all 20 drives, you'll have seen parts of Southern California that most of your friends and neighbors have never heard of, let alone explored.

You'll also know what's being lost as areas develop and might care a bit more when you hear of a new development going in here or there.

### A Few Words On Driving Safety

A nice drive in the country usually involves driving on a two-lane road. Be

**Lonely road in Anza-Borrego Desert State Park.**

**Nate Harrison Grade rises from Pauma Valley to Palomar Mountain.**

aware that most of the roads in isolated areas aren't up to modern standards.

Since the advent of the automobile early in the last century, highway standards have changed greatly. Modern designs include paved shoulders, or breakdown lanes. Curves are banked so gravity helps vehicles. Blind curves are eliminated wherever possible.

That's one reason freeways are easier to drive than country roads.

Most of these drives are on roads less traveled, which means less money for improvements. Many are not much more than paved versions of farm roads dating to the 19th century or earlier. Some aren't paved at all.

Driving on these road requires extra vigilance, so here are some things to remember:

• Drive only as fast as you feel safe and certainly don't exceed the speed limit.

**Rosarito Beach in Baja California.**

• Be aware of what's in front of you. The driver coming around that blind curve might be straddling the center line, leaving no room for your vehicle.

• Be aware of what's behind you.

If there's a line of cars behind you, pull over as soon as it's safe and let them pass. Driving is much more enjoyable when you're not being tailgated.

• If you don't like sharp curves, avoid the drives in this book that have twisting roads.

• Don't overdrive your vehicle. An SUV doesn't handle as well as a Porsche; don't try to keep up with a sports car or motorcycle unless you're driving one.

The driving enthusiast can find these roads more enjoyable just because of the challenge. If you're an average driver, in an average car or SUV, make sure safety comes first.

**How To Use This Book**

This book is aimed not only at the weekend explorer but at the driving enthusiast. Many of us enjoy driving and even find it relaxing (unless we're stuck in traffic and/or commuting).

On these roads you'll find other enthusiasts... convoys of Corvettes, pods of Porsches, and a whole host of Harleys.

The chapters in this book are starting points for your exploration of our great region. They're a travelogue of what I saw along the way, something to whet your appetite for the road.

Each drive has some interesting historical tidbits and a few gems of information. I've also included a few spots to stop, but most of the non-driving exploration is left to you.

In a few of the drives, there are also attractions off the route... nearby but worth a visit, perhaps on a second trip around the route.

**View from Fonts Point, Anza-Borrego Desert State Park.**

**Old gas station, Rainbow.**

The chapters also include a discussion of what type of vehicle is best for the drive. Some are best driven in a sport-utility vehicle or truck with high ground clearance. There's just no getting around the fact that a dirt road can have ruts and rocks that will tear up a sports car or a fine road motorcycle.

Some of the nicest roads in the county are largely wasted on a truck or sport-utility, as their suspension systems and high profiles just aren't the best thing for twisting, curving roads.

Boxes in each section give tips on places to go with kids, when to leave the kids at home, camping, horse trails, and other details.

I've also included a "For More Information" section at the back of each drive which lists addresses, phone numbers, and Web sites for the attractions discussed.

### And Some Thanks...

No project of this size could be completed without a lot of help. My appreciation goes to tour guides who helped me explore new roads: Delena Cozart, Leticia Frieze, Faith Holt, Marc Jaffe, Jim Means, Bertha Sandoval, and Bill Swank, plus all of the folks in the old Miata gang.

Robin Maydeck and Lynne Carrier put their sharp eyes on the text, and Greg Lambert somehow got a good picture of me to put on the cover.

And finally, thanks to Mark Maynard, the automotive editor of the *San Diego Union-Tribune*, who back in 2000 had the courage to begin printing driving columns by a rusty writer.

Enjoy the drives and I hope I see you out on the road.

## Section 1

# Classic Drives

### Traditional San Diego Area Routes

**E**very region has its classic, must-drive roads and San Diego's no exception. These are the places that locals have been taking out-of-town guests since the days of the horse and buggy.

In San Diego County, I've picked five of these drives: the Classic Coastal Route, Del Mar to Point Loma; Lakeside to San Pasqual via Ramona; my dad's favorite rubbernecker route through Rancho Santa Fe and on to Escondido; SR-94 from Rancho San Diego to Boulevard; and Cuyamaca and Julian.

The drives also have a few interesting twists, such as the tour through La Jolla's Muirlands neighborhood; a dirt road (Boulder Creek Road) that's an alternate way to Julian; and the Highland Valley/Bandy Canyon roads combo from Ramona to San Pasqual.

My brother-in-law, a mountain man from Nevada who disdains

cities, visited San Diego for the first time a couple of years ago. We took him on the beach tour, during which he smiled politely as we sat in traffic on Mission Boulevard or looked at the urban vista from Point Loma.

But he was shocked at the Rodeos to Rhinos drive, with the aroma of cows and chickens taking him back home. He also wanted to come back and hunt in some of the wide-open spaces; I hope he checks first to see if that's legal.

That's the best thing about driving around San Diego county. The country roads are, typically, amazingly close to home. And I'm always shocked when locals — even natives — haven't been there.

A few years back, I took — rather, dragged — a friend on a Sunday afternoon drive through Rancho Santa Fe.

Then a twentysomething San Diego native, she was yelling at me to drive slower (yes, my dad's 15 miles per hour — in the Miata, no less) so she could see the mansions on "The Ranch." I was embarrassed, as usual, to drive that slowly, but was more embarrassed for her — a native, who had never been to The Ranch.

If you only take these five drives, you'll have a great overview of San Diego County and have driven some challenging and fun roads.

Be sure to clean the windshield.

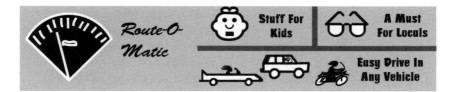

## Drive 1

# It's All Relative

### The Classic San Diego Beach Tour

**We've all had it** happen... relatives or friends are in town and you're on the hook for the Grand Tour. So where to go? Most folks want to visit the beach. La Jolla is a famous destination. The bay and Point Loma are also must-sees.

Today's drive is the route I like to take when Aunt Mildred and Uncle Walter come to town. Get an early start as it's a tad long at nearly 50 miles and, with stops, will take a full day. Along the way are plenty of places to eat, curb-side views of exclusive homes, great scenery, stop-and-stretch spots, and a good sampling of our local life styles.

First, get out of town and head up to Del Mar. Via de la Valle runs

### Distance

- About 48 miles, depending on side trips.

- Lots of stops along the way can use up time, so make sure you're at Cabrillo National Monument before 3:30. It closes at dusk.

DRIVE 1

**Stratford Building in Del Mar.**

past the Del Mar Fairgrounds and Racetrack; here's a chance to inject Hollywood into the discussion.

The track was opened by Bing Crosby, Pat O'Brien, and pals back in 1937 and continues to pack 'em in during its short, 43-day racing season each summer. During the 40s, 50s, and 60s, luminaries such as Jimmy Durante, Desi Arnaz, and J. Edgar Hoover took vacations at the pari-mutuel windows.

Down on the coast is Camino Del Mar. Until the early 1960s, this was the main highway between San Diego and Los Angeles; today, Historic Highway 101 markers run from Del Mar to Oceanside. The *San Diego Union-Tribune*'s Logan Jenkins has documented the highway's history; check SignonSanDiego.com for the complete text.

**C**oast Boulevard goes through the beach front Del Mar neighborhood and past the old Del Mar train station. When they didn't take their own private rail cars, celebrities in the 30s and 40s would hop off Santa Fe's *San Diegan* here and catch a cab to the track. Amtrak and Coaster trains now stop at Solana Beach.

Downtown Del Mar has great shops and restaurants. The 1927-

**Santa Fe Railroad, later Amtrak, stopped here in Del Mar.**

vintage Stratford Bulding at 15th and
Camino Del Mar is a delight; a history
hall is filled with photos of celebrities at
the track in the good old days and other
Del Mar nuggets. Bully's, a classic red-
boothed steak house, is next door.

Next, head south to Torrey Pines,
where the spectacular view of the beach
and cliffs is something you'll only get in
California. Just before going up the hill,
turn right into the state park. Take the

## Stuff For Kids

- Hiking in the Torrey Pines State Reserve.
- Beaches and train watching in Del Mar.
- Whale watching, fishing, and old seafaring history at Point Loma.

twisty grade (once the main highway) up to the visitor center,
which was originally a lodge for travelers on the way between San
Diego and Los Angeles.

**B**ack on North Torrey Pines Road, stops can be made at the
hotels and Torrey Pines Golf Course (home to the PGA
Buick Invitational Golf Tournament) along the cliffs. At Genesee Av-
enue/UCSD, be sure to make the right turn to stay on Torrey Pines
Road.

UCSD includes the historic Scripps Institution of Oceanography,
established 1909 (well before the university). The Birch Aquarium
is a great place to learn about the sea and the work of the institute;
go one block past our turn at La Jolla Shores Drive to visit the
aquarium.

Down the hill to the beach we go. This was another route of the
old Coast Highway, replaced in the 1920s. It's hard to imagine

Model T Fords get-
ting up and down La
Jolla Shores Drive,
but then a century
ago, a trip to Los An-
geles might take two
days or more.

The Shores offers
a great park, beach,
and a quaint shop-
ping/dining district.
If you didn't grab
breakfast in Del Mar,

**Main highway crossed this bridge until 1960s.**

try the Cheese Shop.

Back on Torrey Pines Road, you're probably in a bit of a traffic jam. Don't worry "TP Road" just has a lot of traffic.

On to downtown La Jolla and the Cove. Cave Street takes you past the recently restored Cave Curio Shop to the beach and park. If you can find parking, spend some time walking around this beautiful area.

**U**p the hill is downtown La Jolla. Along Prospect Street, Girard Avenue, and adjacent streets are some of the most exclusive shops and restaurants anywhere. The La Valencia Hotel has been at the center of it all since the 20s and is still known for frequent celebrity visits. Hang out at the Whaling Bar and you might have your own sighting.

Now we're headed up into the hills to rubberneck at some of San Diego's most exclusive homes. Be careful driving, especially on Hillside Drive, as the road is extremely narrow. Follow the directions

**Old lodge at Torrey Pines is now the visitor center.**

**Torrey Pines State Park lodge/visitor center has ocean view.**

carefully and you'll be at the top of Mt. Soledad, where on a clear day you can almost see forever.

After taking in the view, it's back on the home tour through the Muirlands and down to Bird Rock. Calumet Park offers a great spot to get out of the car and stretch after the twisting and curving ride down from Mt. Soledad.

On Mission Boulevard, we're in Pacific Beach. Each beach community has its own character, and PB is known for its concentration of college students. A right turn down any street off of Mission will put you at the beach; restaurants and bars are concentrated on Mission and Garnet Avenue. My cousin Bertha might have liked the rowdy bars; if yours doesn't, choose carefully.

**M**ission Beach starts at the Catamaran Hotel and is more densely developed because it lies on a narrow isthmus between Mission Bay and the Pacific.

At Belmont Park, Mission Boulevard, and West Mission Bay Drive, don't miss

*On The Road*

- Traffic can be heavy throughout the route.
- Be sure to keep your eyes on the road despite the spectacular scenery.
- Old highway leading to Torrey Pines Lodge is twisty. Watch for pedestrians and bicyclists.
- Take it slow through narrow streets in La Jolla's residential neighborhood.

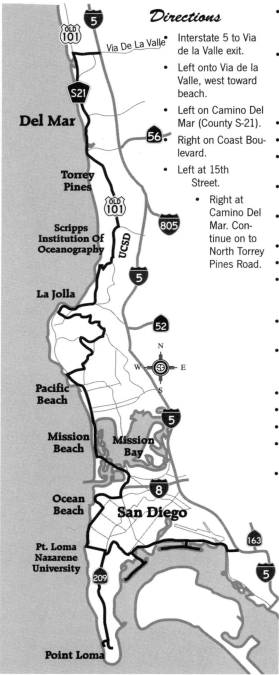

## Directions

- Interstate 5 to Via de la Valle exit.
- Left onto Via de la Valle, west toward beach.
- Left on Camino Del Mar (County S-21).
- Right on Coast Boulevard.
- Left at 15th Street.
  - Right at Camino Del Mar. Continue on to North Torrey Pines Road.
- Keep right at Genesee Avenue intersection to continue on Torrey Pines Road.
- Right at La Jolla Shores Road. For side trip to Birch Aquarium, continue to next intersection, Expedition Way and follow signs.
- Right at El Paseo Grande.
- Right at La Vereda.
- Left at Avenida de la Playa.
- Right at La Jolla Shores Drive.
- Right at Torrey Pines Road.
- Right at Prospect Street.
- Right at Coast Boulevard.
- Left at Girard Avenue. Continue on Girard at Prospect Street.
- Left at Torrey Pines Road.
- Right at Exchange Place. Continue onto Soledad Avenue.
- Right at Hillside Drive.
- Left at Via Siena.
- Right at Via Capri.
- Left at Soledad Road (Mount Soledad).
- Exit Mt. Soledad onto La Jolla Scenic Drive South.
- Right at Nautilus Street.
- Left at Muirlands Drive.
- Left at La Jolla Mesa Drive.
- Right at Linda Rosa Avenue. Continue onto Forward Street.
- Left at Calumet Avenue.
- Left at Sea Ridge Drive.

DRIVE 1

- Right at La Jolla Boulevard. Continue onto Mission Boulevard at Loring Street.
- Left at West Mission Bay Drive.
- Take Sunset Cliffs Boulevard exit.
- Right at West Point Loma Boulevard. Continue onto Spray Street.
- Left at Brighton Street.
- Right at Abbott Street.
- Left at Newport Street.
- Right at Sunset Cliffs Boulevard.
- Left at Hill Street.
- Right at Catalina Boulevard. To visit Point Loma Nazarene University, turn right at Lomaland Drive; check in with guard. To Cabrillo National Monument, continue onto Cabrillo Memorial Drive.
- Exit monument.
- Left at Cabrillo Road to lighthouse, tide pools.
- Right at Cabrillo Memorial Drive. Continue onto Catalina Boulevard.
- Right at Cañon Street.
- Left at Rosecrans Street.
- Right at Shelter Island Drive. Keep to the right to circle Shelter Island.
- Exit Shelter Island.
- Right at Scott Street.
- Right at North Harbor Drive.
- Right at North Harbor Island Drive. Keep right to circle Harbor Island.
- Right at North Harbor Drive.

the Giant Dipper roller coaster. Built in 1925, restored and reopened in 1990, it's one of the few remaining vintage wooden coasters.

Then it's through Mission Bay Park (past a couple of sport-fishing operators, if you want a real detour) and over the San Diego River to Ocean Beach. Some say this area is proudly stuck in the 1960s and I guarantee you'll see a vintage VW microbus on your tour. Antique shops line Newport Avenue.

**Mount Soledad memorial.**

To the south, Sunset Cliffs Boulevard rides the Pacific's edge. Several parking lots allow stops to take in the spectacular view without holding up traffic.

Up Hill Street to Catalina Boulevard and we're in the Point Loma neighborhood. Point Loma Nazarene University is built on the site of the Point Loma Community of the Theosophical Society, a spiritual center built by Katherine Tingley as the 19th century came to a close. If you decide to visit, tell the security guard you want directions to the coastal access view area.

The Cabrillo National Monument and Ft. Rosecrans include the National Cemetery. The old lighthouse and monument at the tip of the point celebrate San Diego's history

**View of Bird Rock from Calumet Park in La Jolla.**

and ecosystem.

The old lighthouse was built in 1855, but it was quickly found to be too high to be effective. To ship captains, its light sometimes looked like a star or was lost completely in the fog. The "new" lighthouse, which continues in operation today at the bottom of Cabrillo Drive, opened in 1891. It is not open to the public.

Further on Cabrillo Drive are the tide pools. Docents are on hand much of the week to tell all about the fragile coastal ecosystem and the role the pools play in the coastal chain of life.

Back on the road, head down Cañon Street to Rosecrans Street and we're on the home stretch. Loop around Shelter Island, then Harbor Island, to experience these two areas created from fill available when the bay was dredged to accommodate larger ships. Shelter, the older of the two islands, has a Polynesian theme, while Harbor offers great views of downtown. Hotels, boat rentals, and restaurants abound.

In between are Fishermens Landing (more sportfishing) and Point Loma Seafood (a great restaurant), as well as the remnants of the Naval Training Center and Lindbergh Field. Any sailor who took basic training at the center will remember the USS *Recruit*, a replica ship used for exercises. The center is being redeveloped into shopping, housing, hotels, and other uses.

Past Lindbergh Field and we're downtown. Our route ends at Grape Street where, if Aunt Cora and Uncle Charlie are tired, you can head home via I-5. Otherwise, enjoy downtown: the Embarcadero, Little Italy (on India Street), and the Gaslamp Quarter.

San Diego has as many facets as a cut diamond and we've seen just a few today. I always recommend taking out-of-towners to the mountains and desert as well, and hope one of the Weekend Driver trips will be their road map to learning more about our wonderful little corner of the world.

## *For More Information*

### Parks & Other Places To Visit

- **Del Mar Thoroughbred Club,** 2260 Jimmy Durante Blvd., Del Mar, (858) 755-1141. *www.dmtc.com* Offers thoroughbred racing for just 43 days during late summer and early fall, off-track betting throughout the year.

- **Del Mar Fairgrounds,** 2260 Jimmy Durante Blvd., Del Mar, (858) 755-1161. *www.delmarfair.com* Annual San Diego County Fair runs in June. Other events held throughout the year.

- **City of Del Mar.** *www.delmar.ca.us* Official Web site has links to local businesses.

- **Torrey Pines State Reserve,** (858) 755-2063. *www.parks.ca.gov* and search for Torrey Pines; volunteer organization, *www.torreypine.org* Reserve protects the Torrey pine tree, a native of the area; also covers beach area.

- **Torrey Pines Golf Course:** 11480 North Torrey Pines Road, La Jolla, (800) 985-4653. *www.torreypines golfcourse.com* Home of PGA tour events; is

**Proudly stuck in the 1960s is Ocean Beach.**

**Dramatic Sunset Cliffs, weathered by Pacific Ocean.**

one of few municipally owned courses on the tour.

- **University of California, San Diego,** 9500 Gilman Dr., La Jolla, (858) 534-2230. *www.ucsd.edu* The university's grounds are in a eucalyptus forest planted early in 20th century.

- **Scripps Institution of Oceanography**, 862 La Jolla Shores Drive, La Jolla. *www.sio.ucsd.edu* Famous worldwide for its scientific research, is today part of UCSD.

- **Birch Aquarium**, Scripps Institution of Oceanography, 2300 Expedition Way, La Jolla, (858) 534-3474. *www.aquarium.ucsd.edu* Aquarium is Scripps Institution's primary public outreach venue.

- **La Jolla Historical Society,** 7846 Eads Ave., (858) 459-5335. Small museum includes exhibits on the history of this exclusive coastal community.

- **Point Loma Nazarene University,** 3900 Lomaland Dr., San Diego, (619) 849-2200. *www.ptloma.edu.* On the site of Katherine Tingley's Theosophical Society, it is today a private liberal arts college.

- **Cabrillo National Monument,** southern terminus of California 209, (619) 557-5450. *www.nps.gov/cabr* One of the busiest national monuments in the nation, the site offers spectacular views of the ocean and San Diego region on clear days. Don't miss the old lighthouse.

- **Point Loma Sportfishing,** (619) 233-1627, 1403 Scott St. *www.pointlomasportfishing.com* Center for sportfishing boats offering day and half-day trips.

- **San Diego Unified Port District,** (877) 224-4229. *www.thebigbay.com* District governs San Diego Bay; Web site includes information on port tenants and attractions.

### Restaurants and Hotels

- **Brigantine Del Mar,** 3263 Camino Del Mar, (858) 481-1166. *www.brigantine.com* Local seafood restaurant offers view of race-track. Scallops were my grandma's favorite.

- **Bully's:** Del Mar, 1404 Camino del Mar. (858) 755-1660. La Jolla, 5755 La Jolla Blvd., La Jolla, (858) 459-2768. *www.bullys.signonsandiego.com* Neighborhood steak houses famous for prime rib, and red naughayde booths.

- **Hilton La Jolla Torrey Pines**, 10950 North Torrey Pines Road, La Jolla. (858) 558-1500. *www.hilton.com* Newer hotel known for its mission-style architecture and furnishings, with great views of adjacent golf course and coastline.

- **The Cheese Shop**, 2165 Avenida de la Playa, La Jolla, (858) 459-3921. A locals' favorite for fantastic sandwiches and sidewalk dining in La Jolla Shores neighborhood.

- **La Valencia Hotel,** 1132 Prospect St., La Jolla, (858) 454-0771. *www.lavalencia.com* Historic hotel sits high above La Jolla Cove; Whaling Bar and restaurant are good spots for celebrity sightings.

- **Catamaran Hotel**, 3999 Mission Blvd., (858) 488-1081. *www.catamaranresort.com* Nautical themed hotel on Mission Bay is just across the street from the ocean.

Coast Guard lighthouse at Point Loma's tip has been operating since 1891.

- **Point Loma Seafoods,** 2805 Emerson St., (619) 223-1109, *www.plsf.com* Fresh seafood dishes, sandwiches, and salads have been served by the Christianson family for more than 40 years. Here's a tip... you order first, *then* get your number.
- **Pizza Nova,** 5120 North Harbor Dr., San Diego, (619) 226-0268. Family-friendly but also for couples, offers wood-fired pizza, pasta, and salads at reasonable prices. Upstairs offers dining with a great view of the bay.
- **Bali Hai Restaurant,** 2230 Shelter Island Dr., San Diego, (619) 222-1181. *www.samchoysbalihai.com* Polynesian kitch from the 1960s has been revamped with updated menu.
- **Tom Ham's Lighthouse,** 2150 Harbor Island Dr., (619) 291-9110. *www.tomhamslighthouse.com* Local landmark has working lighthouse on the roof.

### Other Information Sources

- **The *San Diego Union-Tribune*:** The paper's Web site includes a archives of columnist Logan Jenkins' series on old Highway 101. *www.signonsandiego.com*

Fisherman's Memorial, Shelter Island.

## *Drive 2*

# Rodeos to Rhinos

### *Lakeside to San Pasqual*
### *Through Ramona and the Back Country*

**The treats of a drive** in the country aren't only visual, they can also be aromatic. The smells on today's drive — everything from oranges and hay to, well, essence of dairy farm and chicken ranch — are waiting for you.

So, keep those windows down, because today we go from east to north the back way, driving from Lakeside, home of the Rodeo Grounds, to San Pasqual, home of the Wild Animal Park.

This is a great drive for those out-of-town guests who believe that San Diego is just one giant asphalt

### *Distance*

- About 50 miles.
- Driving takes one to two hours, depending on duration of stops. Start early and spend the rest of the day at the San Diego Wild Animal Park.

DRIVE 2

## Stuff For Kids

- Events at Lakeside Rodeo Grounds.
- Parks, picnics, and hiking along the way.
- Native American history at the Barona Museum.
- Family eats in Ramona.
- Fun, twisting curves on Highland Valley Road.
- Close-up cows and orange trees.
- History at the San Pasqual Battlefield Monument.
- San Diego Wild Animal Park.

## Stuff For Adults

- Barona Casino.
- Wine tasting at Orfila Vineyards.

**Stelzer Park is a cool oasis.**

jungle… we don't have any country like they have "back home."

My brother-in-law is one such skeptic and he was shocked at how quickly the pavement disappeared. So, be amazed.

Head to Lakeside in San Diego's East County, a onetime resort that's now home to horses and gentry.

Your first sight is the Lakeside Rodeo Grounds at Mapleview and Highway 67, home of International Professional Rodeo Association events.

From the Rodeo Grounds, visit the lake in Lakeside, Lindo Lake. The boat house, circa 1889, remains from the days when Lakeside was a resort community. A racetrack was once adjacent to the lake; the legendary Barney Oldfield set a world speed record here in 1907. Today, it offers picnicking and fishing.

**The fun driving begins** as Wildcat Canyon Road climbs to Ramona through the Barona Indian Reservation. It is one of the most beautiful routes in the county.

Corrals greet drivers, but the canyon itself quickly swallows the highway. The first of three county parks is two miles up on the right. Louis A. Stelzer Park, named for the land's donor, was built with the disabled in mind. Picnic facilities, rustic campsites, hiking trails, and play equipment for all are offered.

Five miles up the road are the Oak Oasis and El Capitan wilderness parks, with camping and hiking available.

After a few more twisty-curvys, the road straightens and suddenly it's Las Vegas. At the giant sign, take a left to the Barona Valley Resort, run by the Barona Band of Mission Indians. Stop by and try your luck.

The Barona Museum is just north of the casino and worth a stop. Today's casino operators, one of the San Diego County Kumeyaay tribes, are descendants of the men and women that met the first European settlers.

Continue north as Wildcat Canyon Road gently twists through the reservation, allowing even the driver to enjoy the scenery. Eucalyptus and oak trees create cool canopies over the highway; beyond are golden rolling hills crowned by craggy peaks. Cattle are in the meadows and occasionally on the road, so be alert.

## On The Road

- Scary twisting turns on Highland Valley Road.
- Sometimes heavy traffic on Wildcat Canyon Road south of Barona Casino.
- Lovely, fragrant drive through orange groves in San Pasqual Valley.
- Not-so-lovely fragrant drive through dairy farms in other parts of San Pasqual Valley.
- Route is entirely paved.

Near the valley's top is the Barona Speedway and Drag Strip. A quarter-mile clay track and 1/8th-mile paved drag strip, the facility has races on Saturday nights from April to October. This is auto racing in its most basic form — no pricy NASCAR teams here. It's worth a visit on race nights.

**Barona Museum is just a mile north of the casino.**

**Wildcat Canyon Road twists through Barona reservation.**

Seven miles past the casino is San Vicente Road. A left turn heads through the corrals and ranchettes into Ramona. Horses, chickens, and dairy cattle in this area also add a unique bouquet.

This rural hamlet has picked up some suburban features over the years but still keeps its bucolic charm. At the intersection of 10th (San Vicente Road changes its name for the last few blocks) and Main streets, turn right to Ramona's original business district. Downtown has a collection of old country cafes and shops, most retaining their back country charm, and the Town Hall is being restored. Get a good cheeseburger and a great slice of pie at the Kountry Kitchen, 826 Main St.

South of 10th is urban Ramona and dreaded strip malls. But have no fear, bucolic byways are just ahead.

### *Backyard Byway*

- An "In Your Backyard" drive that surprises even longtime locals.
- Experience the county's mountains and valleys, towns, and farms, all in a couple of hours.

After turning onto Highland Valley Road, you're back in farm country, climbing on the outskirts of the Ramona Valley. A mile down the road you'll see the Fund For Animals Wildlife Rehabilitation Center, a hospital for nature's own.

This stretch of Highland Valley Road is a bit unique... long straightaways and occasional 90-degree turns. Don't miss the right turn at Archie Moore Road (3.5 miles since you left Highway 67) to stay on Highland Valley.

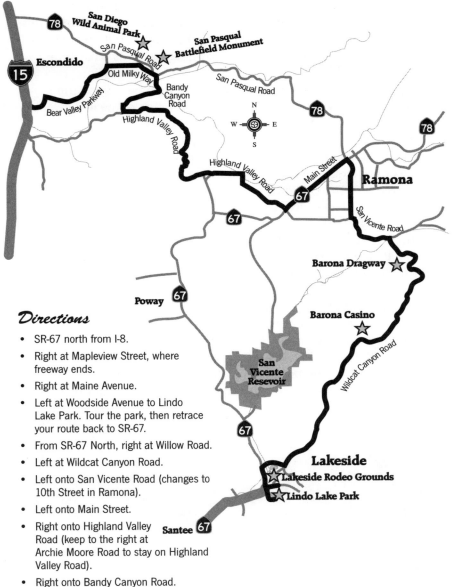

## Directions

- SR-67 north from I-8.
- Right at Mapleview Street, where freeway ends.
- Right at Maine Avenue.
- Left at Woodside Avenue to Lindo Lake Park. Tour the park, then retrace your route back to SR-67.
- From SR-67 North, right at Willow Road.
- Left at Wildcat Canyon Road.
- Left onto San Vicente Road (changes to 10th Street in Ramona).
- Left onto Main Street.
- Right onto Highland Valley Road (keep to the right at Archie Moore Road to stay on Highland Valley Road).
- Right onto Bandy Canyon Road.
- Left onto San Pasqual Road (SR-78).
- Left onto Old Milky Way.
- Left onto Via Rancho Parkway.
- Left onto Bear Valley Parkway to I-15.

DRIVE 2

The most challenging part of the route for the driver is next. Highland Valley makes some great hairpin turns as it goes over the hill and down to the next canyon. On a hot day, you'll notice it cooling off as you descend into the craggy gorge with its oak canopy.

**N**ext up, a touch of rural France: hedgerows. Smell the orange groves that are on the other side of the leafy walls. Watch for another crop grown here, palm trees.

As quickly as they arrive, the hedgerows disappear and it's nothing but orange and avocado groves. The strong orange aroma brings back memories of an earlier time in Southern California when old U.S. 101 sliced through miles of citrus in Orange County.

At nearly 10 miles from Ramona's Main Street, make a right onto Bandy Canyon Road to the San Pasqual Valley. It twists a bit through hills and dairy farms to SR-78.

San Pasqual Valley is a very rural place, to be sure, but also part of the City of San Diego. Most of the land was bought by the city years ago over water rights issues and is now an agricultural preserve, leased to dairy farmers and ranchers. Don't miss Bert Verger's spread on your left, but watch your speed, since there can be children playing around the Verger compound.

At SR-78, make a left. Watch for "San Pasqual Store, Beer and Antiques," just past the bridge. They have water and munchies here, in addition to antiques, rocks, and, of course, beer. Just don't drink any antique beer.

Ahead is San Pasqual Battlefield Museum, which chronicles the

**Hedgerows line Highland Valley Road.**

**San Pasqual Valley vista from the Battlefield Museum.**

1846 Mexican War skirmish here. Worth a visit, its exhibits tell of the valley and the battle between U.S. General Stephen Kearny (as in Kearny Mesa) and the Californios lead by Major Andres Pico.

A mile south, turn left at Old Milky Way and cruise by more farm houses. It's more enjoyable than 78, which has been widened and straightened to handle traffic from the San Diego Wild Animal Park, on your right.

To go to the Wild Animal Park, turn right at Via Rancho Parkway/San Pasqual Road and follow the signs. The park is a spectacular place, especially when it is open on summer nights. Taking the monorail at dusk is a must.

**H**eading southwest on San Pasqual Road, check out Orfila Vineyards, a working winery and tasting room. Continue on San Pasqual Road to conclude the drive.

Now you're in San Diego's North County, having gone the "back way" to Escondido. Freeways could have gotten you there faster and easier, but this route traverses some of the county's most scenic hills and canyons, giving you the view — and aroma — of another side of San Diego.

### For More Information

- **Lakeside Rodeo Grounds**, SR-67 and Mapleview Drive, (619) 561-4331. www.lakesiderodeo.com. Call for event schedule.
- **Lindo Lake Park**, library, community center, and Historical Society museum, (619) 443-3696. Historical Society, (619) 561-1886.

**Old Milky Way is a good alternative to busier San Pasqual Road.**

- **County Parks**, Stelzer, Oak Oasis, and other parks in the area, (619) 694-3049. Web site: *www.sdcounty.ca.gov/parks/*.

- **Barona Casino and Museum**, 1932 Wildcat Canyon Rd., Lakeside, (619) 443-2300, *www.barona.com*. Indian casino, hotel, golf course, and museum on reservation.

- **Barona Speedway**, Wildcat Canyon Road, north of Barona Casino and south of San Vicente Road, (619) 669-1303, *www.baronaspeedway.com*. Auto racing on a quarter-mile dirt track.

- **Barona Drag Way,** 1750 Wildcat Canyon Road, north of Barona Casino, (619) 445-3559, *www.baronadragstrip.com*. One-eighth-mile paved drag strip offers summer racing.

- **Fund For Animals Wildlife Rehabilitation Center**, 18740 Highland Valley Rd., Ramona, (760) 789-2324. Guided tours are available at 11 a.m. and 2 p.m. Saturdays and Sundays, holidays excluded. *www.fundwildlife.org*

- **San Pasqual Battlefield Historic Park**, 15808 San Pasqual Valley Road, Escondido, (760) 737-2201. *www.parks.ca.gov* and search for San Pasqual. Visitors center open 10 a.m. to 5 p.m. Friday-Monday.

- **San Diego Wild Animal Park**, 15500 San Pasqual Valley Road, Escondido, (760) 747-8702. *www.sandiegozoo.org*. Preserve includes animal exhibits, a train through open enclosures, and other activities. Operated by San Diego Zoological Society and open daily, including evenings during summer months.

## *Drive 3*

# Roadways of the Rich and Famous

### *Cruising Through Fairbanks Ranch and Rancho Santa Fe to Funky Del Dios*

**R**obin Leach would feel right at home on this route. We'll start out in one of the county's fastest growing communities, Carmel Valley, and cruise through two of the wealthiest areas in the nation — Fairbanks Ranch and Rancho Santa Fe — and after 30 miles or so end up in funky Del Dios.

Begin at Interstate 5, taking SR-56 exit. One of these days, this

**Distance**

- About 40 miles.
- Allow time to explore shops in Fairbanks Ranch and Rancho Santa Fe.

### Stuff For Adults

- Great views of great big homes.
- Shopping in Rancho Santa Fe and other spots.

road will connect with its other half in Peñasquitos, but today it ends a few miles east of I-5, dumping traffic on Carmel Valley Road then bumpy Black Mountain Road.

Hardly improved since the days when trucks used it to carry fresh tomatoes, strawberries, and other veggies to market from the nearby fields, Black Mountain Road is now filled with deluxe sport utility vehicles and upscale sedans motoring to the freeways. A strawberry stand is a remnant of the past.

The vegetable fields are mostly gone, giving way to oversized, million-dollar tract homes on undersized lots. As an Easter Sunday treat, I took my mom on this route and she asked who was buying all the condos she saw from Carmel Valley Road.

Sorry, mom. The dwellings crammed together aren't condos. They're single family homes, wall-to-wall. So much for the wide open spaces in the country.

At Rancho Santa Fe Farms Road, turn left to Fairbanks Ranch. Silent movie icon Douglas Fairbanks and his wife, Mary Pickford, had a weekend escape here.

Today, Fairbanks Ranch is home to exclusive estates with front gates, long driveways, pink stucco, and Spanish-tiled roofs. Check 'em out, but don't drive too slowly as the natives (and their security patrols) can get restless. I once took an out-of-town guest on a cruise here and we were followed for several miles by a

**Eucalyptus grove covers Rancho Santa Fe.**

**Downtown Rancho Santa Fe includes historic buildings.**

private security guard in a police-style vehicle. Still, it's fun to see how the other one percent lives and, after all, these are public streets (the gates and more guards tell you when they aren't public streets).

**N**ext up is the Helen Woodward Center, one of the county's premier animal-rescue facilities. Open daily to visitors, it's next door to the Fairbanks Ranch shopping area.

In a new community, I always like to pick up a copy of the local newspaper or real estate circular. They're available at this center and help to add some local flavor to the drive. Seven- and a few eight-figure homes are listed, so if you're in the market for a new flop, make a deal.

After the turn at Apajo, don't miss the left to Calzada Del Bosque, which is a bit hard to see. Hidden here is the Chino family farm's Vegetable Shop, 6123 Calzada del Bosque, which is one of the premier vegetable markets in Southern California. Chefs from the finest restaurants in the region — from as far away as Los Angeles — line up early in the morning for the pick of the day.

Continue on Calzada Del Bosque across the San Dieguito River, busy Via de la Valle, and up into "The Ranch," Rancho Santa Fe.

*On The Road*

- An easy route for whatever vehicle you drive.
- Bumpy Black Mountain Road will have a lot of traffic until SR-56 is completed.
- Watch directions carefully for turns through residential areas.
- Del Dios Highway is very busy.

DRIVE 3

An enclave of exclusive homes on large lots amidst a grove of eucalyptus trees, The Ranch is one of the wealthiest communities in the nation. Although not a city of its own, The Ranch is largely governed by "the Covenant" — condo-like deed restrictions on the property — and The Rancho Santa Fe Association.

**The Inn at Rancho Santa Fe.**

Before the homes, there was the Santa Fe Railroad, which planted the fast-growing eucalyptus to use as railroad ties. That didn't work out, so the area was turned into an exclusive escape.

The trees make this portion of the drive most pleasant, even on hot days. Speed limits are mostly 35 mph or less, and by sticking to the posted limits you'll have a chance to get a peek at some of the homes. Everything in The Ranch is as discreet as possible — homes are usually hidden from the street by shrubs or trees. Gates are there, but low-key, unlike the in-your-face security in Fairbanks Ranch; of course, that makes it harder for drive-by snoops.

Round about on Rambla de las Flores and up to La Granada, where a right turn will take you along the edge of the Rancho Santa Fe Golf Club. Follow the course to Avenida De Acacias; turn right to The Inn at Rancho Santa Fe and the rest of downtown.

Park and walk around, as downtown Rancho Santa Fe is a real treat. The Rancho Santa Fe Historical Society has a great section on the local Web site detailing the history of The Ranch and these structures in particular.

## *Rubbernecker Special*

- Don't forget to yield to faster traffic on these routes.
- Beautiful homes are around every corner.
- Embarrass your kids by driving really slow through the neighborhoods.

### Directions

- Interstate 5 to SR-56.
- East on SR-56 to end.
- Continue on Carmel Valley Road to Black Mountain Road.
- Left on Rancho Santa Fe Farms Road.
- Left on Rancho Diegueño Road.
- Right on San Dieguito Road.
- Left on El Apajo.
- Right on Via De Santa Fe.
- Left at Calzada Del Bosque; continue onto Rambla De Las Flores.
- Right at La Granada (S-9).
- Left at Avenida De Acacias.
- Left at Paseo Del Delicias.
- Left at El Montevideo.
- Right at Lago Lindo.
- Right at El Camino Del Norte.
- Left at Del Dios Highway (S-6).
- Right at Rancho Drive, continue onto Lake Drive.
- At about Beech Lane, right into Lake Hodges park.
- Back at Lake Drive, turn right (north).
- Right at Via Rancho Parkway to Interstate 15.

Architect Lillian Rice designed The Inn for the Santa Fe Railroad. In the 1920s it provided a place for visiting railroad executives and prospective home buyers. By the 1930s, according to the Historical Society, it was an in-spot with the Hollywood crowd — Errol Flynn, Bette Davis, and Jimmy Stewart among others. Today, its restaurant has breakfast, lunch, and dinner at surprisingly reasonable prices.

Just east is the Rice-designed civic center,

DRIVE
3

**Wild mustard blooms on hills in spring.**

with the original school, town houses, apartments, and commercial buildings now filled with shops, restaurants, and banks.

Back on the road, head out Paseo Delicias to a short loop by the San Dieguito Reservoir, one of the county's least known lakes. The area also has quite a few Ranch homes that are really ranches — raising horses, avocados or other crops. Then head back to Del Dios Highway on El Camino Del Norte.

As you turn left to Del Dios Highway, look straight ahead for a great view of some still-open rolling hills. In the spring, these hills are covered with flowering wild mustard, creating a neon-yellow feast for the eyes.

Quickly, Del Dios Highway leaves The Ranch and heads over the rugged hills to Lake Hodges; its dam is the first thing you'll spot. During wet years, water flowing over the dam's spillway creates a spectacular waterfall. In dry years, the lake is well below spill level.

This long, skinny reservoir was built in 1917 to help development in Rancho Santa Fe. Now part of the San Dieguito River Park, the lake meanders through the San Dieguito River gorge to I-15. If you believe tall tales, a Loch Ness-style serpent named Hodgee lives in the lake.

**Horse trail is next to Rancho Santa Fe Golf Course.**

DRIVE
3

The small community of Del Dios lines the western shore, its small stucco homes shaded from the near-year-round heat by trees of all variety. A couple of decent restaurants bookend the community: Del Dios

**Dam at Lake Hodges rises from valley.**

Country Store and Cafe on the east; and on the west, Hernandez Hideaway, once owned by the purported inventor of the margarita.

Del Dios has all the charm of a seasonal lakeside resort. Lake Drive runs along the water's edge, with a couple of access areas providing places to picnic and fish. On the west end of the lake, across from Hernandez Hideaway, is the Lake Hodges Aquatic Center. On the east is the city park; turn right at the Del Dios Country Store to the park area. I didn't see any sign of Hodgee during my visit.

Head back up Lake Drive to Via Rancho Parkway and Interstate 15 to end today's drive.

From I-15 south you catch a glimpse of this serpentine reservoir and the rugged hills you've just crossed. Home to the rich and famous, just regular folk, and possibly a monster name Hodgee, the county's central coast region is a treasure of sights and well worth a drive.

## *For More Information*

- **Carmel Valley** community information: see the Web site, *www.cvsd.com.*
- **Fairbanks Ranch Country Club,** 15150 San Dieguito Road, Fairbanks Ranch, (858) 259-8811, *www.fairbanksranch.com.* Private golf course and club was site of 1984 Olympic Equestrian Endurance Event, two years before it opened. At the club's entrance, bronze sculpture "Victory's Gate" commemorates Olympics.
- **Helen Woodward Animal Center,** 6461 El Apajo Road, Fairbanks Ranch, (858) 756-4117, *www.animalcenter.org.* The 12-acre, nationally

recognized cen-
ter has adoption
kennels, stables,
a therapeutic
riding program,
and pet boarding
facility, as well as
small-animal and
equine hospitals.

Popular park area at Lake Hodges.

- **The Vegetable Shop**, 6123 Calzada del Bosque, Fairbanks Ranch, (858) 756-3184 for recorded farm stand information. Known for its fresh vegetables grown on the adjacent farm. Operated by the Chino family.

- **Rancho Santa Fe Association,** (858) 756-4372. Governing body for covenant area.

- **The Inn at Rancho Santa Fe,** 5951 Linea Del Cielo, Rancho Santa Fe. (858) 756-1131, *theinnatrsf.com.* Historic hotel, restaurant in the heart of The Ranch.

- **Rancho Santa Fe Historical Society,** Web site, *www.rsf.com/areahist.html..*

- **Mille Fleurs Restaurant,** 6009 Paseo Delicias, Rancho Santa Fe. (858) 756-3085, *www.millefleurs.com.* Renowned restaurant on The Ranch.

- **San Dieguito River Park,** office, The San Dieguito River 18372 Sycamore Creek Road, Escondido, (858) 674-2270, *www.sdrp.org.* Government agency is preserving the river area from mountains to sea.

- **Hernandez Hideaway,** 19320 Lake Drive, Del Dios, (760) 746-1444. Great Mexican restaurant near the shore of Lake Hodges.

- **Lake Hodges Aquatic Center,** 20110 Third Place, Escondido, (760) 735-8088, *lakehodges.net.* Center offers a variety of activities at lake.

- **Lake Hodges**, Lake Drive, Escondido, *www.sandiego.gov/water/recreation/hodges.shtml*

- **Lake Hodges Scientific Research Center,** *www.hodgee.com.* Humorous site discusses sightings of Hodgee, the Loch Ness-style animal that reportedly resides in lake.

- **Del Dios Country Store,** 20154 Lake Drive, Del Dios, (760) 745-2733. Restaurant and store has good food, music in the evening.

## *Drive 4*

# Out 94 Way
### *Heading East on South County's Main Street*

**A** smooth, fast connection to the east has been a dream of San Diego boosters since the Spaniards set up the first European settlement here in 1769.

In the way are the rugged and sometimes cruel mountains that lead to an equally cruel desert.

One of the earliest routes east is the subject of today's drive — since the 1930s known as California Highway 94. Histories of the area are incomplete, but it appears this was the first route east that was entirely in the United States, existing before the inaugural stagecoach run in 1870.

Over the 54 miles from the Jamacha Junction to Boulevard, the highway snakes

### *Distance*

- About 54 miles from Rancho San Diego to Boulevard. Straight-through drive takes about 90 minutes.

- Allow another hour's drive for return trip over Interstate 8.

**Old Sweetwater Road bridge is open for cyclists, hikers, and horses.**

through the mountains and valleys of southeastern San Diego County, and communities with names like Jamul, Dulzura, Potrero, and Campo, close to Mexico before ending in Boulevard. There are plenty of places to eat, plus parks, campgrounds, and lots of twisting, rugged driving.

## For The Kids

- Explore funky old cars at Simpson's Garden Town Nursery.
- Plan a day for fun train rides at San Diego Railroad Museum.
- Spectacular scenery as road twists through gorges.
- Camping, picnicking at Potrero Regional Park.
- Explore Tecate, a very different Mexican town than Tijuana.

## Not For The Kids

- Roadhouse cafes along the way are more adult-oriented, unless your kids are old enough for beer and pool.

**T**ransportation history also abounds. In addition to a route possibly dating back more than 150 years, there are auto, truck, and train museums along the way.

It's also one of the few highways with its own club and Web site; the Highway 94 Club meets regularly and has lots of historical tidbits on its Web site. Shirley Bowman has written a great history of the route and the people that created it. We'll keep Lou Stein's *San Diego County Place Names* handy for other historical details.

If you want to go the full length of today's 94, head east from the end of G Street in downtown San Diego. Originally called the Crosstown Freeway, this stretch was one of San Diego's first, opening in

1957. Stay with SR-
94 as it swings east
at the SR-125 inter-
change to the "Casa
De Oro Connector."

The scenic
stretch begins after
the freeway ends,
with a turn onto
Campo Road at an
intersection once

Classic Fords are on display at Simpson's.

known as Jamacha Junction. The first reminder of the age of this
route is the old Sweetwater Road bridge, preserved to the right of
the span built in 1987. The bridge has been preserved for walking
or biking; if you have time, turn off at Singer Lane and enjoy the
river view.

**T**hings are becoming more built-up on this twisty road to
Jamul, but they are still pretty rural. Pens hold horses and
other farm animals, while the biggest fences keep human teenagers
corralled at Steele Canyon High School.

Jamul is a wonderful, close-in stop for fresh vegetables (Steele
Canyon Produce), to dine or spend the afternoon. Shopping for a
saddle? Check out the several tack shops along the way.

For green thumbs and car buffs, Simpson's Garden Town Nursery
is a must see. Right in downtown Jamul at Campo and Proctor Valley roads, owner Lee Smith has two barns and much of the nursery

grounds filled with
more than 50 vin-
tage autos, pickup
trucks, boats, travel
trailers, and as-
sorted automobilia.
Car clubs hold
shows on the
grounds.

Stein credits the
native Kumeyaay
with naming Jamul:

Car clubs find Simpson's a popular gathering spot.    it could be "foam or

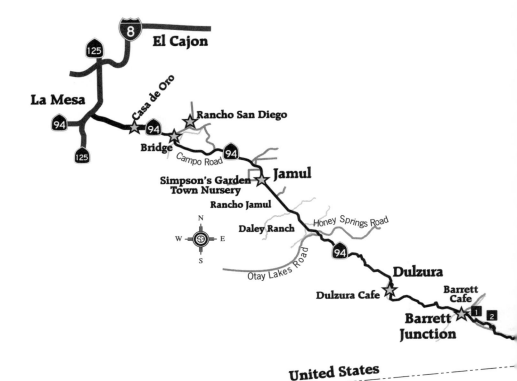

### On The Road

- Highway is full of twists and blind curves.
- Can be scary at times.
- Watch speed on downgrades.
- Traffic can be heavy from La Mesa to Tecate.
- Narrow, two-lane road begins at Jamul.
- Very few services along the way. Fill up the tank in Rancho San Diego.

lather," "place where antelope drink water" or "slimy water."

Beyond town, civilization thins even more as drivers roll through the valleys that are home to Rancho Jamul and the Daley Ranch, longtime cattle lands. The valleys are gorgeous and green in years with normal rainfall, but dry spells can leave them pretty brown.

Past Otay Lakes Road, the real challenging driving begins. Traffic is heavy at times as trucks headed to Tecate can clog the road. The hairpin turns, narrow lanes, and disappearing shoulder also add to the thrill.

Dulzura is the next hamlet on the way.

## *Directions*

- Take SR-94 from SR-125 junction east to Campo Road.
- Right at Campo Road.
- Left at Barrett School House Road. **1**
- Continue onto Barrett Smith Road. **2**
- Left onto Campo Road (Highway 94).

- Optional Tecate, Mexico visit: Right at SR-188 to border.
- Potrero Park: Left at Potrero Valley Road **3**. Right at Potrero Park Road. **4**
- Left at Ribbonwood Road to Interstate 8 and return to San Diego.

The Dulzura Cafe, a great spot for burgers and cold beverages, is one of several surviving roadhouses along SR-94. Out front is a portico where gas pumps once sat.

Cross through another mountain ridge and we're at Barrett Junction, home of Leon Herzog's cafe, another classic road house known for its fish fry. A turn here will take you to the lake, which has limited fishing.

### A Must For Locals

- Exploring this part of the county opens your eyes to the rugged mountains to the east.
- History is around almost every curve in the road.
- The scenery ain't bad, either.

**J**ust past are remnants of old 94 that are still drivable. It's hard to see, but after crossing the Cottonwood Creek bridge, start up the hill and take the left at Barrett School Road. Wind around onto the eastern segment of Barrett Smith Road and the old highway. The western segment of Barrett Smith Road is no longer connected as the bridge over Cottonwood Creek is long gone.

DRIVE 4

Dulzura Cafe, left, and post office.

The pavement is a bit rough, but the extra twisting grade is marked by some vintage mileposts, a sure sign of the old highway. It offers a spectacular view of the Potrero Creek gorge that's only partially visible from today's 94.

This stretch of road is used occasionally as an "extreme sports" course, hosting international racing events. Watch out for cyclists, skateboarders, and the occasional street luge.

**R**ejoin the highway at the top of the grade. If you missed the turn at Barrett School Road, make the left here and loop back; it's well worth the detour.

The valley quickly disappears as 94 climbs along the edge of Potrero Creek and the junction with SR-188, the two-mile link to the border. It's a great side trip to Tecate, considered more of a typical Mexican town than its bustling neighbor, Tijuana. The namesake Tecate Beer brewery towers above the skyline.

Back on 94, we're headed to Potrero, Spanish for "meadow or pasturing place," according to Stein, who notes it was first settled by Maine sea captain Charles McAlmond in 1868. Spacious Potrero Regional Park has picnic areas, camping, and RV hookups. The Potrero Store and Cafe is also a great spot to stop for refreshment, as summer heat is intense in the back country.

Road twists as it leaves Dulzura.

Back on the highway, the San Diego and Arizona Railroad makes its first appearance as a "Subway Ahead" sign alerts drivers to the narrow underpass. Yet another attempt to connect the markets of the east with the San Diego Bay,

Barrett Smith Road follows old highway alignment.

the railroad was completed by sugar magnate John D. Spreckels in 1919. Washed out by storms in the 1970s, the latest plan has it reopening in the next couple of years.

This stretch of track is used by the San Diego Railroad Museum, headquartered up ahead in Campo. Saturday and Sunday, 16-mile train rides are run to the east; special trains run to Tecate several times a year.

Passengers exit a tour train at Campo.

Watch for the turn to the museum just before crossing the railroad tracks and the old Gaskill Brothers stone store. The brothers defended the store in a classic Wild West shoot-out with Mexican desperadoes in 1895; today it is open as a museum and antique store.

The wide valley at Campo was home to Camp Lockett, where the Army's famous Buffalo Soldiers black cavalry regiment trained. German and Italian

DRIVE
4

### Camping

- Potrero Regional Park has tent sites, RV hookups.
- Several private campgrounds are also along the route.

prisoners of war were held at the base during World War II.

Just past Campo is Cameron Corners, a onetime stagecoach stop named after Thomas Cameron, an early settler, reports Stein. Egg and horse ranches dot the area.

Towering above the valley is the old feldspar mill, now home to the Motor Transport Museum, a private antique truck museum. Feldspar, a mineral used in production of porcelain items such as toilets and sinks, was mined in nearby Hauser Canyon, ground, and shipped out on the railway. The mill closed in 1949.

**A** **high bridge** marks the last appearance of the railroad as Highway 94 gently winds through ranchettes toward the Campo Indian Reservation. The tribe has built the Golden Acorn Casino on the other side of the property, adjacent to Interstate 8.

The highway then hooks north at the town of Boulevard toward Interstate 8. In 1963, the year the team won its only American Football League championship, the San Diego Chargers held their preseason training camp here.

With the freeway in sight, drivers can decide how to get back to San Diego. After a day of mountain driving, a nice smooth trip back on I-8 might be just the ticket, retrace your route back over SR-94, or cruise old U.S. 80, which parallels Interstate 8 most of the way.

Either way, you've had a great trip through some of San Diego County's most challenging and historic territories.

**Old feldspar mill is now home to truck museum.**

## *For More Information*

### Parks, Museums, and Places To Visit

- **Simpson's Garden Town Nursery**, 12925 Highway 94, Jamul, (619) 669-1977. This 25-acre nursery has a wide assortment of plants, plus antique cars, travel trailers, and other goodies throughout. Two car barns have restored vehicles ranging from the Model T Ford to AMC Pacer. Car clubs and other activities are scheduled most weekends. By the way, Simpson's denies it has a phone number; above listing gives a recorded message only.

- **San Diego Railroad Museum**, 31123-½ Highway 94, Campo, (619) 478-9937, *www.sdrm.org*. Train rides on weekends, plus railroad memorabilia is on display at the original San Diego and Arizona Railroad depot. See Web site for rail fan trip schedule.

- **Motor Transport Museum**, 31949 Highway 94, Campo, (619) 478-2492. A private antique truck museum; call for operating hours.

- **Potrero County Park,** 24800 Potrero Park Dr., (877) 565-3600. Pleasant county facility offers RV hookups and tent camping, picnicking, and other day uses. *www.sdcounty.ca.gov* and search for park.

### Other Information Sources

- **Highway 94 Club**: Organization dedicated to issues relating to SR-94 route from Sweetwater Road to Boulevard, *www.hwy94.com*.

- **Jamul Indian Village:** Information on the Native American tribe in Jamul, *www.jamulindianvillage.com*.

**San Diego and Arizona Railroad crosses Highway 94 on high bridge.**

- **Kumeyaay Nation:** Information on the Native American tribe in San Diego County, *www.kumeyaay.com*

- **Weather and Other Mountain Information:** Provided by Potrero radio station, 103.3 "The Box." *www.rockingthebox.com/wx.htm*

### Restaurants, Shops

- **Dulzura Cafe:** 16985 Highway 94, Dulzura, (619) 468-9591. Classic roadhouse serving burgers, beers, and billiards. Favorite for car and motorcycle clubs. Closes at 2 p.m.

- **Barrett Junction Cafe:** Barrett Lake Road and Highway 94, Barrett Junction, (619) 468-3416. Famous fish fry continues to pack 'em in, also open for lunch. *www.barrett-junction.com*

- **Potrero General Store**, 25125 Highway 94, Potrero, (619) 478-9208. After the long drive from San Diego, a great spot to stop for cold drinks.

- **Potrero Cafe,** 25125 Highway 94, Potrero, (619) 478-2697. Call for operating hours.

Cattle graze near Campo.

| Route-O-Matic | Stuff For Kids | Rubbernecker Special |
| --- | --- | --- |
| | SUV Recommended | |

## Drive 5

# Indians, Miners, Boxers, Ocean View

### Through Cuyamaca, Julian, Boulder Creek

**O**ne of the most beautiful, lush forests in the county traces its roots and preservation to the Kumeyaay, the Native American tribe that has called this area home for more than 2,000 years, and the Ralph M. Dyar family, who helped secure their homestead as a public park.

*Distance*
- About 60 miles.
- Allow 40 minutes from central San Diego to Descanso.

Cuyamaca is that special place, and today's drive will take us through the park, to a historic lodge just outside Julian, into the old mining town, and back south through working cattle ranches that are largely untouched by development.

DRIVE 5

**Old Dyar ranch house is now Cuyamaca Rancho State Park museum.**

Head east on Interstate 8 to the Descanso/SR-79 turnoff, about 45 miles east of San Diego. Here, unhurried drivers can jump on a long stretch of Old Highway 80, what's left of the former U.S. 80 that was San Diego's link east before Interstate 8.

We're just going up the road a bit, where today's SR-79 heads north into Cuyamaca.

This state park is a real gem in our part of the country. The valley — headwaters of the Sweetwater River — was named by the Kumeyaay *Ah-ha-Kwe-ah-mac*, "The place where it rains."

**For The Kids**

- Great places to hike, camp, picnic, and explore nature in Cuyamaca Rancho State Park.
- Chance to show the folks Camp Cuyamaca, the school camp, located next to the park headquarters.
- What kid doesn't like Julian apple pie?
- It's fun watching mom or dad drive on a dirt road.

The rain, terrain, and altitude have produced carpeted meadows, as well as oak and pine forests. It's also home to the second-highest point in the county, the 6,512-foot Cuyamaca Peak. For visitors, there are hiking and horseback riding trails, picnic areas, campgrounds, and great vistas. It's also a popular spot to visit during winter snows.

The amenities begin almost as soon as you leave Descanso. The road twists and rises in elevation, while the forest begins to envelop the highway.

Green Valley, at elevation 3,957, is the

DRIVE 5

first major park area, with camping, picnicking, and hiking. Generations of San Diegans have enjoyed this oasis along the Sweetwater River.

But if you've never visited the park before, head just a couple of miles further north to the museum and park headquarters.

The museum is located in the former home of the Dyar family, who owned the property from 1923-33. They sold the property to the state — at half price — so a park could be developed.

Exhibits also highlight the Kumeyaay, who spent the summer here (with winters in the desert or coastal foothills). They resisted the intrusions of the Spaniards and later Mexicans, fighting several battles from 1782 until a treaty was signed in 1837. Uprisings were still reported over the next few years, until 1855, when James Lassator bought 160 acres from the Kumeyaay near Green Valley.

If you grew up in San Diego, the location might look familiar... Camp Cuyamaca, visited by thousands of sixth graders and other county school kids for more than 70 years, is next door.

To really explore the park, pick up one of the excellent brochure/maps. Select a few things for today; there's plenty to explore for many return visits.

On my trip, I also stopped at the Old Stonewall Mine, near the lake at the north edge of the park. One of the largest gold mines in Southern California, it produced during San Diego

*On The Road*

- Unpaved Boulder Creek Road is well worth the bumps and ruts.

- Twisting curves on SR-79 and Engineers Road are fun for a sports car, but higher ground clearance can be needed on Boulder Creek Road.

- Traffic can be heavy on weekends on SR-79. Be sure to yield to faster drivers.

**There's not much left of the Old Stonewall Mine.**

**Lake Cuyamaca is a nice place for fishing.**

County's gold rush era, 1870-90. The gold discovery brought thousands of Europeans and Chinese to the area, finally sending the remaining Kumeyaay to reservations.

The mine once employed more than 200 workers, supporting a town at Cuyamaca. In 1892, the mine was flooded out and abandoned, along with the town. Resort homes and a few businesses supporting fishing at the lake are along SR-79 today.

There's a pair of restaurants at the lake. During my visit, I stopped for lunch at the Lake Cuyamaca Restaurant and Store, which has a surprisingly different menu full of Austrian specialties.

The dam at Cuyamaca is the second-oldest in California, built in 1888. The Lake Cuyamaca Park and Recreation District keeps it stocked and oversees the concessions, which include the store and restaurant, a bait shop, cabins, and camping, fishing, and boating.

Heading up the west side of the lake, look for the left turn to Engineers Road. This twisting grade winds up to Pine Hills, our next stop today.

In 1912, the lodge and surrounding community were established as a mountain retreat for San Diego's elite. The rustic main building has a dining room and bar, with a spacious lobby overlooking the pine forest.

The adjacent building, painted barn red, is today a dinner theater but was built in

*Rubbernecker Special*

- Fantastic vistas around every turn.
- Lots to see in Julian.
- Hidden Boulder Creek Road is another secret road.
- Engineers Road is a driving enthusiasts' favorite.

## *Directions*

- Interstate 8 east to SR-79. Follow SR-79 to left off of Old Highway 80.
- Left on Engineers Road.
- Right on Boulder Creek Road.
- Right on Blue Jay Drive.
- Right on La Posada Way to Pine Hills Lodge.
- Left at Blue Jay Drive.
- Return to Boulder Creak Road. Right turn to SR-78/79 and Julian.
- Right at SR-79 south, leaving Julian.
- Right at Engineers Road.
- Left at Boulder Creek Road.
- Left at Oak Grove Drive.
- Left at Viejas Grade Road.
- Right at Riverside Drive.
- Right at SR-79 to I-8.

**78** Julian

Boulder Creek Road

Pine Hills Lodge

**1**
**2**

Engineers Road

**79**

Inaja Indian Reservation

Boulder Creek Road

**1** Blue Jay Drive
**2** La Posada

**Lake Cuyamaca**
**Old Stonewall Mine**

**Paso Picacho Campground**

N
W — E
S

**Cleveland National Forest**

Boulder Creek Road

**Cuyamaca Rancho State Park**

**Park Headquarters and Museum**

**Green Valley Campground**

Oak Grove Drive

Cuyamaca Highway

**Descanso**

Riverside Drive

**79**

Old Highway 80

**OLD 80**

**8**

1926 as a training facility for boxer Jack Dempsey. Then-owner Fred Sutherland was a buddy of Dempsey and brought the fighter here to tune up for his second bout with Gene Tunney. Dempsey lost the fight, but the barn remained.

When Dave Goodman owned the property in 1979, he turned the gym into a dinner theater, which continues in operation today. A renovation of the lodge was completed after Scott and Debra Kinney took over in 1998. Cabins are available for overnighters and the lodge continues as a popular spot for weddings and other mountain social occasions.

As long as you're here, head a couple of miles northeast to the mountain town of Julian, where San Diegans have been going to es-

DRIVE 5

**Boxer Jack Dempsey's old gym at Pine Hills.**

cape since the gold rush days.

First on the way is the Julian "suburb" of Wynola, which has a couple of good restaurants (including the Julian Pizza Express), stores selling apples, plus the Orfila Winery tasting room and Helga O Art Center (at the old Manzanita Ranch store site). Over curvy Wynola Road is the Menghini Winery, which boasts that it's the only vintner that actually produces wine in Julian.

Downtown Julian can be a traffic and parking nightmare. A suggestion: Park in the pay lots, located at 4th and B or on A Street just off of Main Street. Then, enjoy the stroll through the shops and restaurants that line Main and Third streets. Don't forget to hike up C Street to the Eagle and High Peak mines.

When you've had enough apple pie, antiques, and Julian fun, head south on SR-79. It will take you back to Lake Cuyamaca and Engineers Road, which is such a great drive we'll do it again.

Retrace your drive back to the Pine Hills Fire Station. This station is an important protection for the area, which was very close to the spectacular fires around Julian in 2002. It's also adjacent to the Inaja Indian Reservation, one of the county's smallest and most remote (no casino here!).

At the fire station, veer to the left for the trip back to Descanso over unpaved Boulder Creek Road. This road would bore serious rock crawlers; I had no problem negotiating it in my Miata.

Boulder Creek of-

**Downtown Julian still has its wild west look.**

fers spectacular views of the valleys and mountain peaks descending to the coast. It's also a jumping off point for several hiking trails in this, the west-central portion of the Cleveland National Forest.

Watch for cattle grazing along the way; evidence suggests Boulder Creek

**Cattle ranch operates off of Boulder Creek Road.**

Road was originally built to access the local ranches. A few improvements have been made through the years, including a Works Progress Administration (WPA) project from 1937.

As on any dirt road, keep alert for ruts and rocks, and vehicles coming the other direction, as Boulder Creek Road is narrow and has a number of blind curves. There are, however, plenty of spots wide enough to stop and just take in the view.

On a clear day, the view goes all the way to the ocean, and the first vista is just a couple of miles south of the Pine Creek Fire Station. It's pretty amazing to gaze to the southwest and see the San Diego Bay, Pacific Ocean, and Coronado Islands shimmering on the horizon.

Directly west is Ramona, about 4-5 miles as the crow flies. The hiking trails heading that direction are marked with Forest Service signs; some follow fire roads. Portions of the area are private property, so keep to the marked trails.

For the most part, the trees end at the timber line, about two miles south of the fire station. Unlike lush Cuyamaca, with its forests and meadows, this area is mostly Southern California chaparral. The bush provides a furry covering over the sharp hills, with the occasional boulder poking through. Otherwise, the coastal sage scrub, manzanita, and other native plants run as far as the eye can see.

The road occasionally dips into the gorges, fording a few streams. Natural oaks grow where there's water, sometimes provid-

**Hiking trail leads from Boulder Creek Road.**

ing a canopy to cool hot drivers on sunny days.

After twisting and grinding on the dirt for more than 10 miles, we're in the community of Descanso, where the snow usually ends in the winter. At the intersection of Riverside Drive, there's a small store and cafe for refreshment at the end of the trail.

Then it's back on Old Highway 80, the interstate and San Diego.

For anyone living in central San Diego, Cuyamaca is just about the closest and best mountain recreation center. Whether it's camping, hiking, picnicking or just a drive in the country, this is truly a vacation in your own back yard.

## For More Information

- **Cuyamaca Rancho State Park**, 12551 SR-79, Descanso, (760) 765-0755. Park includes spots for picnicking, camping, hiking, and general day use. *www.cuyamaca.statepark.org*

- **Inaja Memorial Picnic Area**, Cleveland National Forest, State Highways 78/79, east of Santa Ysabel, (760) 788-0250.

- **Pine Hills Lodge**, 2960 La Posada Way, Julian, (760) 765-1100, *www.pinehillslodge.com*.

- **William Heise County Park**, 4945 Heise Park Road, Julian, campground reservations: (877) 565-3600, *www.sdcounty.ca.gov/parks/*.

- **Julian Pizza Express**, 4355 SR-78, (760) 765-1004, *www.wynolasprings .com*. Pizza restaurant with artist-designed fireplace.

- **Menghini Winery**, 1150 Julian Orchards Drive, Julian, (760) 765-2072. Small winery in meadow has tasting and picnic areas.

- **Orfila Vineyards**, State Routes 78/79 in Wynola, 13455 San Pasqual Road in Escondido, (760) 738-6500, *www.orfila.com*. Branch of San Pasqual winery at site of old Manzanita Ranch store.

- **Julian Chamber of Commerce** Web site, *www.julianca.com*

## Section 2

# The Best Driving

**Great Hills and Valleys, Twists, Curves, and Views Throughout San Diego County**

**A**sk sports-car owners or motorcycle tourers where their favorite road is and you're likely to get a description of something with hairpin turns and scary twists… anything that gives an adrenaline rush.

For sport-utility drivers — at least those that use them for sport, rather than utility — the route is probably paved with something other than concrete or asphalt.

For these folks, the best roads aren't in urban areas, they're in the mountains or valleys and San Diego County has some of the best roads of this kind anywhere in the world.

So, tighten the seat belt or the strap on your helmet and head out over the next five drives: Japatul Road, east from El Cajon to I-8

near Descanso; a historic dirt road, Black Canyon Road; Mount Laguna The Back Way over mostly dirt roads; History on Pala Road, a twisty route that has a thousand years of stories; and Cruisin' Old 101, the coast highway from Oceanside to Solana Beach.

This section includes several unpaved roads. Several are public roads, maintained by the county, but unpaved. Others are trails within a National Forest or State Park.

If you don't own a SUV, rentals are available. Most of the major car rental firms now advertise SUVs such as the Ford Escape or Jeep Liberty. Simple... just fork over that credit card, and you're ready to head to the desert.

Not so fast. Rental firms don't like you taking their vehicles off road. Most don't even like you to take them off paved roads.

And your insurance might not be valid either, as some have clauses excluding any damage suffered off the pavement. Plus, when you return the vehicle, the agency will go over it with a fine-tooth comb if they suspect you've been off road... and might do a detailed inspection just as a matter of course.

So, if you don't own a 4x4, your best option might be to make friends with your neighbor with the mammoth sport-ute. Start by offering to pay for the gas.

Take your camera along as there are great views all along these drives, visiting places like Mount Palomar, the Japatul Valley, Mesa Grande, Pine Valley, Guatay, Leucadia, and Carlsbad.

Have a great time.

## Drive 6

# Via Japatul

### Over Crest, Through Harbison Canyon and Dehesa to a Great, Wide-Open Highway

**O**ne of the best roads in the county.
How else do you describe the Dehesa Road-Japatul Road-Japatul Valley Road stretch running from the bustling Sycuan Casino to Interstate 8?

It's one of those roads that enthusiasts dream of, one of those roads where you can see a street rod, sports car or sports bike — or all three — tearing around the curves... on a weekday. Or, the only other vehicles on the road are from the Border Patrol.

It has all of the things that make a great driving experience: sharp curves, gentle curves, straightaways long enough to pick up

### Distance

- About 30 miles.
- Very few straightaways once drivers leave Interstate 8.

DRIVE 6

Nancy Jane Park in Crest is a great picnic spot.

**Stuff For Adults**

- A casino and lots of twisty driving might bore youngsters.
- There's fishing at Loveland Reservoir, but it's a long hike to the shore.

speed, gentle grades, not much traffic (at least after you pass Sycuan), and a great view.

Its only flaw is that it isn't long enough. But, today we'll add enough at the beginning of the drive that it should make for a fun afternoon for the driver. For you passengers, just hang on and watch the nice view.

First a few sites before we hit The Road.

The itinerary takes us up the hill from El Cajon, over La Cresta Drive from Interstate 8 to the community of Crest (take the Greenfield Drive exit from I-8). This mountaintop hamlet of small homes has a couple of nice picnic places, including Nancy Jane County Park. There's also the Coyote Country Cafe — last stop for latte — and a couple of convenience stores. Enjoy the view from this Mayberryesque community.

**L**eaving Crest, follow Mountain View Road down the hill to Harbison Canyon. Like many rural byways, Mountain View Road has been suburbanized over the last few years, gaining curbs, gutters, and sidewalks as well as being smoothed out a bit. But don't worry, it will kink up a bit near the bottom — where the name changes to Frances Drive — and there's plenty more twisties to come.

Frances Drive meets up with Harbison Canyon Road near the community's helipad. It was installed several years ago to provide access during emergencies in this rugged community.

According to Lou Stein's indispensable book, *San Diego County Place Names*, the canyon was named after John Harbison, considered the father of Southern California's honey business. He and his 110 bee hives homesteaded the area in 1869, at one point shipping more than 200,000 pounds of honey to Eastern markets.

## On The Road

- Great twists and curves.
- Watch the speed... we don't want any fatalities.
- Traffic is generally light after passing Sycuan Casino.

Today, it's an oak-shaded canyon with small ranchettes. The Canyon Inn, the local watering hole, is one of those classic road houses where everybody knows your name... the regulars give strangers the once-over when they walk in. But, they're a friendly bunch once they decide the out-of-towner's just stopped by for a burger and a cold one.

**Wide open highway east of Sycuan Casino.**

Across from the Canyon Inn is a classic piece of automobilia... an old gas station with a drive-up bay sized for a Model T. The place now dispenses propane and sadly the gas pumps, which probably last sold gas at 19 cents a gallon, are long gone.

At Dehesa Road, turn left and you're on The Road.

Watch for signs

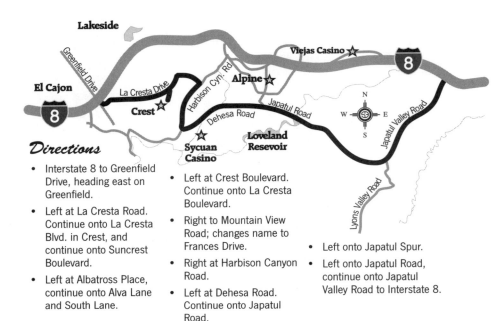

## Directions

- Interstate 8 to Greenfield Drive, heading east on Greenfield.
- Left at La Cresta Road. Continue onto La Cresta Blvd. in Crest, and continue onto Suncrest Boulevard.
- Left at Albatross Place, continue onto Alva Lane and South Lane.

- Left at Crest Boulevard. Continue onto La Cresta Boulevard.
- Right to Mountain View Road; changes name to Frances Drive.
- Right at Harbison Canyon Road.
- Left at Dehesa Road. Continue onto Japatul Road.

- Left onto Japatul Spur.
- Left onto Japatul Road, continue onto Japatul Valley Road to Interstate 8.

to Sycuan Casino and its traffic. Bigger than ever, the casino draws crowds to this area, especially on weekends. Buses and slow-moving land yachts can clog the road; don't worry, though, Sycuan's traffic doesn't last long.

If you haven't been into the casino in awhile, check it out. They've recently completed a major addition and the place looks more like Las Vegas every day. There are also several restaurants and it is your last chance for liquids, as there are no services through the end of the drive.

### Backyard Byway

- This road is hidden behind developments in El Cajon and Alpine.
- Take the drive... you'll be surprised.

**N**ow, let's start the good stuff. Dehesa Road quickly starts to twist a bit. The trees of the valleys soon disappear and you're on the edge of the rugged Sweetwater River gorge. At the junction with Alpine's Tavern Road, the route changes its name to Japatul Road.

One of the major rivers in the county, the Sweetwater runs from near the base of Mt. Laguna all the way to San Diego Bay. Several

**Springtime view of Loveland Reservoir.**

lakes are along the way, including Loveland Reservoir.

This is one of the more isolated lakes in the county. To get there, take the public access trail about five miles east of Sycuan. It's about a half-mile hike down a steep hill to the valley floor, then it can be another half-mile to the water if the lake level is low during drought years.

Hikers will take a well marked but rustic trail. If you decide to fish, pick up a license before arriving as there are no services.

Japatul Road continues east, following the gorge. It's here that you can open it up a bit... but be careful.

The twists are tight but the long straightaways make it fun. Just when you've had enough of the turns, the road straightens out. When the uphill grade gets tiresome, it flattens out. The variety on Japatul Road is what makes it great.

Japatul, according to Stein, is a Native American Kumeyaay term for "place of water" or "fruit of the prickly pear." The valley, which you'll slice through via Japatul Spur, was home to a Kumeyaay village until the 1890s.

Today, the valley is home to a few farms. Japatul Spur is well worth the short detour. The gentle, rocky, rolling hills, and pasture lands dotted with native oaks are somewhat reminiscent of granite-strewn New England farms.

**Rolling route adds to fun along Japatul Road.**

Past Lyons Valley Road there's another name change, this time to Japatul Valley Road. More twists, turns, straights, hills, and dips, and you'll be at Interstate 8. If you're lucky, you'll see a group of landscape painters overlooking Horsethief Canyon.

Sometimes roads are great for what you see along the way; others are great for their topography. The Dehesa-Japatul route has sights for the passenger and challenges for the driver, making it one of the best.

## *For More Information*

- **County Parks**, (619) 694-3049. *www.sdcounty.ca.gov/parks*. Look for information on Nancy Jane Park and other open space.
- **Coyote Country Cafe,** 229 Alamo Way, Crest. (619) 442-5460.
- **Canyon Inn** 550 Harbison Canyon Rd., (619) 445-6583. Biker-friendly watering hole in downtown Harbison Canyon.
- **Sycuan Casino and Resort**, 5469 Casino Way, El Cajon, (619) 445-6002/(800) 2-SYCUAN. *www.sycuan.com*. Full-service casino located off Dehesa Road. Operated by the Sycuan Band of the Kumeyaay Nation.
- **Cleveland National Forest**, (760) 788-0250, *www.fs.fed.us/r5/cleveland* and look for information. Federal forest area that runs from Riverside County to near Mexican border.

## Drive 7

# Dirt Paradise

### Black Canyon Road Turns Back Time

**A**bout 150 miles of unpaved — but maintained — dirt roads exist in San Diego county.

These roads are kept passable by county crews, who regularly scrape the surface to ensure that ruts are kept to a minimum, that gravel and dirt are in the proper proportion, and that the road is passable — most of the time.

So, all of you with four-wheel-drive sport utility vehicles have no excuse to keep those clear-coat paint jobs and leather seats free of mud and dust.

*Distance*

- About 45 miles.
- Allow travel time to Ramona.
- Allow plenty of time for eating and shopping, plus room in the car for bread from Dudley's.

These roads range from truck trails with pretty steep verticals to this cruise, Black Canyon Road, which is twisting but mostly level; it offers some great views into our backcountry's past.

DRIVE 7

**Tight curves mean the possibility of head-on meetings with other drivers.**

I drove this road three times... twice with friends in their sport-utilities (an older, full-sized Ford Bronco and a brand new Mercedes-Benz ML320) and once in my Mazda Miata.

Both of my sport-ute friends are veteran off-roaders and thought the road was a bit easy. It was an adventure in the Miata, but I've bumped through more potholes in downtown San Diego.

So, grab some bottles of water (for you and your passengers) and let's hit the dirt.

Get yourself to Ramona via SR-78 or SR-67, cruise through town to Magnolia Avenue and make a left. At the corner is the old house from Rancho Santa Maria, an original Spanish land grant that once covered all of Ramona and much of the area we'll cover today. The house is still a private residence.

### Stuff For Kids

- Checking out graffiti on the Black Canyon Road bridge.
- Swimming in the creek.
- Cows at Mesa Grande.
- Santa Ysabel Mission.
- Goodies at Dudley's.

Continue north on Magnolia; at Pile Street it becomes Black Canyon Road. A Cleveland National Forest office is on the left; if you're planning on stopping to picnic or hike along the way, get a car permit. Although the road is owned and maintained by the county, most of the land along the way is in the Pine Creek Wilderness area preserve and the forest service requires a parking permit.

After less than a mile, the pavement ends. There will be a few patches of asphalt, but otherwise you're on Nature's Own for the next six miles. Take it easy.

Black Canyon Road climbs slowly to the edge of the canyon. Far below is the Santa Ysabel Creek. Homes disappear and the vistas open up, sights that, for the most part, haven't been scarred by civilization.

### On The Road

- Black Canyon Road is almost all dirt.

- You'll see the Harley folks at the Hideout, but they won't touch dirt roads.

- Lots of history... just when was this road first used?

One of the oldest thoroughfares in the county, Black Canyon Road is shown on an old county map, "Roads and Trails, 1769-1885," at the San Diego Historical Society in Balboa Park. It was used to ferry supplies, cattle, and ranchers from northern communities such as Julian and Warner Springs to the markets in Ramona and San Diego.

I couldn't find a date for the road's original construction, but the histories say the livestock and farming in the area supported the Franciscan mission system, which was mostly in the south and west. The missions were established beginning in 1769, so it is possible this route was established in the 18th century. It hasn't

**Sign notes bridge's history.**

**Crossing the Black Canyon Road bridge.**

changed much since.

The first segments are on the upper edge of the canyon, twisting around the contours. Pay attention to those "Use Horn on One Lane Curves" signs. There isn't much traffic — in the three trips, I only met three cars going the other way. Still, be safe and honk that horn.

**This first stretch is** high above the canyon floor. If you remember the early '60s movie, "It's A Mad, Mad, Mad, Mad World," the terrain looks like what Phil Silvers traversed in his '47 Ford convertible. The good news is that this road is going horizontal along the top of the canyon. Phil was going vertical, losing his oil pan in the process and eventually ending up in a creek. No problems like that today.

*Nature Lovers Ride*

- Great vistas around every turn.
- You'll have to drive slow... this is a dirt road.

There are signs that the Works Progress Administration (WPA) rebuilt some of the highway during the 1930s, but the biggest improvements were made around 1913, when the bridge was constructed over the Santa Ysabel Creek. Designated historic by the County of San Diego, it's worth a stop.

DRIVE 7

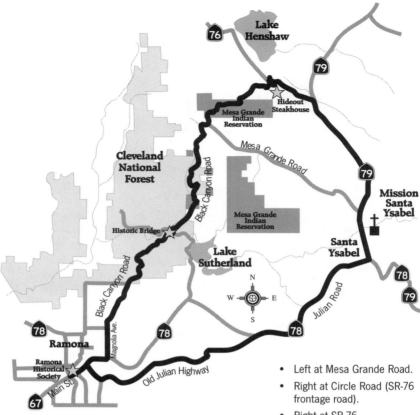

## Directions

- Take your best route to Ramona (SR-67 from Lakeside, or via Poway Road or Scripps Poway Parkway from Interstate 15; SR-78 from Escondido).

- Ramona's Main Street/SR-78 north (changes name to Julian Road).

- Left on Magnolia Avenue (changes name to Black Canyon Road).

- Left at Mesa Grande Road.
- Right at Circle Road (SR-76 frontage road).
- Right at SR-76.
- Right at SR-79.
- Right at SR-78 (Julian Road).
- Left at Old Julian Highway.
- Left at Main Street (SR-78) in Ramona.

A graceful arched curve, the bridge is one of just three remaining designed by William M. Thomas. Dozens of bridges with the "three hinge" design were built around the state early in the 20th century.

According to the county report prepared when the bridge was designated historic, this is the best-preserved example of the three remaining. It is the only one essentially in its original setting — still looking much as it did back in 1913. Located in a gorge of natural oaks that turn golden in the fall, there's even some vintage graffiti

DRIVE
7

**Rugged terrain is unspoiled.**

under the triple arches.

Unfortunately, Mr. Thomas's design isn't up to 21st century seismic standards. The county plans a new bridge for cars, but will preserve the existing span for pedestrian and equestrian traffic.

Black Canyon Road makes a sharp left to cross the bridge; if you go straight, you'll end up at the Sutherland Reservoir. Take the bridge.

**S**it back and enjoy the challenge of the dirt drive for another couple of miles. Be sure to stop at the vistas and look south. The chaparral-covered hills roll into the craggy gorge; rock outcroppings add a little variety to the view.

At about four miles in, the gorge narrows as you're near its top. It's only a few yards down to the creek bed, where there are natural oaks and other dense vegetation... signs of water. Here, the creek flows over rock faces and ponds for most of the year, a rarity in our arid climate.

Folks do come and swim in the cold water, but be careful. If you want to park and check out the swimmin' hole, you'll need that permit from the Forest Service.

One of the park rangers told me that several times a year they have to rescue people who have banged their heads or sustained other injuries. It's nice to know the rangers are there — if you can contact them and afford to wait as long as an hour for help.

In other words, enjoy the outdoors, but remember you're a ways from civilization.

Next up the road is the Mesa Grande Indian Reservation, which you'll drive through in the last segments of the canyon. After a few more twists, the canyon opens up into Mesa Grande.

**B**eautiful grazing lands are filled with contented cattle, with golden grasses punctuated by oaks and rock outcroppings. If you look up to your left into the hills, tailings from mines are visible. These mines continue to produce tourmaline and other gems... and aren't open to the public.

At Mesa Grande Road (about 15 miles since we left Ramona), make a left. This well-maintained paved highway is one we'll cover fully on another drive, but today we'll take it up to SR-76 and Lake Henshaw.

After driving carefully on dirt for the last few miles, you'll enjoy opening it up a bit on Mesa Grande. Still, be careful because there are some nice curves.

There is a bit more traffic on Mesa Grande... not cars, but motorcycles. It is a favorite of the Harley Davidson crowd not only because it's a great road, but because one of the Harleyites' hangouts is at its north end... the Hideout Steakhouse.

Where Mesa Grande Road meets SR-76, follow the line of parked Harleys to the Hideout Steakhouse, a surprisingly friendly oasis.

Harley enthusiasts Ron and Nancy Robinson opened the place in

**Road snakes along canyon sides.**

**Stream flows over rocks even in dry years.**

1999 and operate it only Friday-Sunday.

Friday and Saturday nights, it's a fancy dinner house with prime rib prepared by a "four-star chef," while the daytime lunch menu includes burgers and roast beef sandwiches.

This is a place for the weekend riders like Ron and Nancy, who have been riding "hogs" for many years. During the week, he's a aircraft systems and flight testing consultant for custom business jets.

"When I asked Nancy to marry me, I said, 'Do you want a ring or a Harley?'" said Ron. "She took the Harley."

This place doesn't fit the stereotype of a "biker bar." There isn't even a pool table. And while the clientele are all decked out in fine leathers, they mostly seem to be "Harley hobbyists," working, like Ron, at Regular Jobs during the week and hitting the road on the weekend.

Even if you're not on a bike, it's worth dropping in at the Hideout Steakhouse.

Head south on SR-76 toward our next stop in Santa Ysabel. Make a right at SR-79 about 2.5 miles down the road from the steakhouse, then keep your eye out for Mission Santa Ysabel, just under four miles ahead.

At the intersection with SR-78 is the town of Santa Ysabel, famous for Dudley's Bakery. Folks come from miles around for Dudley's breads in countless varieties. Santa Ysabel also has a couple of antique and art shops, a market, a restaurant, and a branch of the Julian Pie Company.

Antique stores and art galleries line both sides of SR-78, although the area's walkability is hampered by cars blasting through at 65 miles per hour. Worth a visit is the "twig furniture experience" of Curt Bevine's The Giving Tree, where this onetime professional jockey fashions willow branches into chairs, tables, bookcases, and other items for a wild looking living room.

You're missing a treat if you don't leave Santa Ysabel with something... Dudley's bread is fantastic, as are the pies at the Julian Pie Company. The Apple Country Restaurant serves bison burgers and other prime cuts grown at a ranch down the road; what could be fresher?

Head south on SR-78 for another six miles. From here, take a left turn at the Old Julian Highway. It's a nice, twisting drive through ranches and the Ramona "suburbs."

Turn left at Main Street and you're back on SR-78. One last stop is at the Guy B. Woodward Museum of History, operated by the Ramona Historical Society. It offers a vintage look at the Ramona valley with exhibits on days gone by, a library and the Casey Tibbs Memorial Exhibit, dedicated to the late world champion rodeo rider and local resident.

By this time, your sport-utility should be good and dirty. You can

**Cattle graze at Mesa Grande.**

Hideout Steakhouse is a (friendly) biker hangout.

decide if you want to stop in at car wash for cleanup, or drive it around muddy for a few days to show off.

## *For More Information*

- **Cleveland National Forest**, (760) 788-0250, *www.fs.fed.us/r5/ cleveland* and look for information. Federal forest area that runs from Riverside County to near Mexican border.

- **Dudley's Bakery**, 30218 Highway 78, Santa Ysabel, (800) 225-3348, *www.dudleysbakery.com*. The great mountain bakery has been a favorite stop for years.

- **The Giving Tree**, State Highways 78 and 79, Santa Ysabel, (760) 765-0090, *www.willowcreations.com*. Willow furniture created by former professional jockey.

- **Hideout Steakhouse,** 27413 Highway 76, Santa Ysabel, (760) 782-3656. Open weekends and evenings; call ahead. Prime rib and steaks in the evening, burgers during the day.

- **Kountry Kitchen**, 826 Main Street, Ramona, (760) 789-3200. Home cooking and great pies.

- **Guy B. Woodward Museum, Ramona Pioneer Historical Society**, 645 Main Street, Ramona, (760) 789-7644. Honors rodeo star and area history.

National Forest

Scenic: Byway

· SUNRISE ·

## Drive 8
# Back Way to Laguna
### Up and Over the Mountain Via Viejas Grade, Pine Creek Road, and Kitchen Creek Road

**There's almost always** a different way to get from here to there.

Sometimes it's dirt, sometimes it's partially paved and sometimes it's full of potholes.

Today's drive has all of those things.

Going from Alpine to Mt. Laguna is no big deal. Just get on Interstate 8, exit Sunrise Highway (county Highway S-1) and you're there. Maybe a stop off in Pine Valley for an ice cream cone.

You didn't think we were going to take the easy route, did you?

### Distance

- About 55 miles from Alpine to Mount Laguna and back to Pine Valley.
- Allow about two hours for the drive, plus time from your home to Alpine and back from Pine Valley.

DRIVE 8

**Dusty Viejas Grade climbs quickly from valley.**

## Stuff For Kids

- This is an almost all-outdoors drive, so leave the video games at home. Turn off the in-car VCR and leave the windows rolled down to enjoy fresh mountain air.
- Bumpy Pine Creek Road has places to stop and hike.
- Laguna Mountain Recreation Area has more places to picnic, hike, and camp.
- The ice cream in Pine Valley is always a reward.

## Stuff For Adults

- Gambling at Viejas.
- Antique and art shops along Old Highway 80.
- A romantic weekend at Laguna Mountain Lodge or other small hotels, or camping in the Cleveland National Forest.

A map check of the area between Pine Valley and Mt. Laguna shows a couple of roads parallel to I-8 and Sunrise Highway; we're taking them today.

Our 55-mile loop begins east of Alpine, heads up the back way to Descanso then over historic old U.S. 80. After a spell, we head up a back way to Mt. Laguna, then opt for a twisty dirt road down the mountain, and back over Old Highway 80 to Pine Valley.

**A couple of notes:** First, the weather can be severe in San Diego's mountains, so be sure to check the forecast and pack plenty of water. Plan on warm clothes in the winter and sun protection in the summer. Yes, it can snow up here as late as April.

Second, make sure your car, SUV or truck is ready for a bumpy, pot-holed journey. You'll need a vehicle with some ground clear-

DRIVE 8

**Bridge over Pine Creek was built to protect rare frog species. Gate is ahead.**

ance. I didn't take my Miata on this drive, although I did see several folks in standard passenger cars along the way.

*On The Road*

- First dirt road begins at eastern edge of Viejas Indian Reservation.

- Pine Creek Road is rocky and not always in best shape. Be careful.

- Gates can close Pine Creek Road and Kitchen Creek Road. Call the Cleveland National Forest ranger station at to find out if gates are open.

- Stay on marked roads and trails; other roads might be on private property or closed by the Forest Service.

- Buy Forest Service Adventurepass in advance.

**H**ead east on I-8 and take the Willows Road exit, heading north toward the Viejas Casino.

Willows is a busy, two-lane road headed to the tribal casino and adjacent outlet mall. Worth a stop, but maybe on the way back as we're going to take the turn at Viejas Grade, a "Y" intersection a mile or so west of the casino.

This section of the road loops around the northern part of the reservation, home to the Viejas Band of Kumeyaay Indians. Here you'll see what the tribal lands were like before the casino — small homes and farms — although the pre-gambling poverty is gone.

The Viejas Band moved here after the City of San Diego was allowed to purchase the heart of the Capitan Grande Indian Reservation for the El Capitan Reservoir. It

DRIVE
8

**Pine Creek Road winds through natural oak grove.**

was completed in 1934 and is visible from I-8 just east of the Harbison Canyon exit.

The road twists and turns past the Viejas Mission church and cemetery. Pavement ends on the valley's northeastern edge.

Viejas Grade then heads into the mountains, quickly climbing on the rocky side of Poser Mountain. Lou Stein's *San Diego County Place Names* notes that it was named after early settler Heinrich von Poser. A spectacular view of the Viejas valley, Alpine, and San Diego unfolds as drivers traverse the bumpy route to the top. The drop is considerable if you stray off the road, so be alert.

**A**fter about four miles of dirt, the pavement returns near the top of the grade, entering the community of Descanso. A wonderful small community nestled in a ravine, the settlement dates back to the 1880s. Follow the street signs through this residential area, past the Ranger Station and Descanso Town Hall, and on to Viejas Boulevard. Stables in the area offer trail rides.

Loop through Descanso and onto Old Highway 80. Hard to imagine it now, but before Interstate 8 opened in the early 1970s, this was U.S. 80, the route to Imperial County, Arizona, and points east. One lane in each direction through mountain communities such as the one up ahead, Guatay.

DRIVE 8

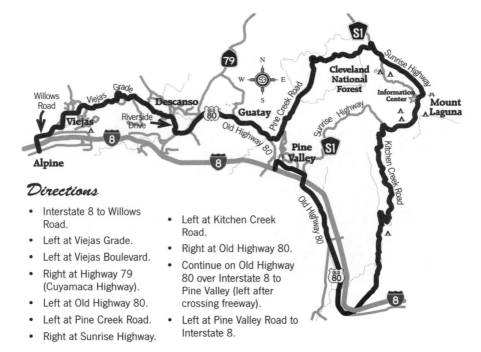

## Directions

- Interstate 8 to Willows Road.
- Left at Viejas Grade.
- Left at Viejas Boulevard.
- Right at Highway 79 (Cuyamaca Highway).
- Left at Old Highway 80.
- Left at Pine Creek Road.
- Right at Sunrise Highway.

- Left at Kitchen Creek Road.
- Right at Old Highway 80.
- Continue on Old Highway 80 over Interstate 8 to Pine Valley (left after crossing freeway).
- Left at Pine Valley Road to Interstate 8.

Stein reveals that Guatay was once a favorite winter home for the Native Americans of the area, ancestors of today's Viejas Band. Nearby is Guatay Mountain, which was thought to be home to a great chief.

**T**ake Old Highway 80 for about three miles. The vintage concrete road's expansion joints will make a slap-slap noise on your tires. Watch out for the next turn, a left onto Pine Creek Road just before Old Highway 80 bridges Pine Creek.

The road runs along the creek, sheltered by the namesake pines. Entering the Cleveland National Forest, a sign points out that the small cottages are summer homes on land leased from the Forest Service.

Here, you'll cross Pine Creek on a nar-

## Nature Lovers Ride

- A great tour of the undeveloped backcountry.
- From arid foothills to lush mountain slopes to the high desert, explore many of San Diego's ecosystems.
- Marked hiking trails run from Pine Creek Road and Sunrise Highway.
- Keep quiet and you might see deer, rare birds, and even endangered frogs.

DRIVE 8

**Beautiful vista from near top of Pine Creek Road.**

row bridge. The $500,000 span opened in January 2001 to protect
the creek bed habitat of the endangered arroyo southwestern toad.
The road originally forded the normally dry bed, squashing the
toads and their eggs.

**J**ust past the homes is a gate that the
U.S. Forest Service closes during
bad weather. Call ahead to the Alpine
ranger station, (619) 445-6235, to check
road conditions.

At about six miles since leaving Old
Highway 80, be sure to make the right turn
at the small sign marked "Pine Creek
Road." Beware... this is shown as "Hidden
Valley Road" on some maps. If you go
straight, you'll end up at Lake Cuyamaca,
but that's for another day.

Another two miles and what's left of the
pavement becomes just another lump next
to a pothole. You'll really want to slow it
down on this stretch so you don't ruin the
suspension on your vehicle. The pines

### Arts and Eats

Spoons get double duty
along this route as eating
utensils and art.

- Several restaurants of
  varying quality are in
  Descanso, Guatay, Mount
  Laguna, and Pine Valley.

- Don't miss having an ice
  cream cone at Frosty
  Burger in Pine Valley.

- Spoons are art at the
  Tryyn Galley, where artist
  Bill Chappelow crafts
  rare woods into cutlery
  lookalikes.

DRIVE 8

have disappeared and you're in an open but rugged area of the Cleveland National Forest.

Up ahead is a sign noting the boundary of the Laguna Mountain Recreation Area. By this time, you're back in the woods, mostly oaks and pines. In the summer, the oaks provide shade from the intense sun; in the fall, their golden leaves are proof we do have changing seasons in Southern California.

The recreation area is full of hiking trails, campgrounds, picnic areas and

Sunrise Highway has a traditional forest look.

other places to enjoy. Another mile and we'll hit Sunrise Highway, county Highway S-1, also designated the Sunrise National Scenic Byway. Oaks and pines also dominate this area, creating a canopy in the spring and summer, a golden tunnel in the fall, and a spooky arch over the road during the winter.

**P**oints of interest are well marked along Sunrise Highway. Up first is Penny Pines, a monument (and Penny Pines plantation) honoring the children and organizations that donate pennies to plant trees in national forests. Two hiking trails are also accessed from this spot.

The information station next to the Mt. Laguna Lodge and Store is a great place to check out everything about the area. The store has supplies and rents cabins at reasonable rates.

DRIVE 8

**Pine grove surrounds visitor center at Mount Laguna.**

Continue south on Sunrise Highway, past the turn for San Diego State University's Mt. Laguna Observatory, and make the left at Kitchen Creek Road. This gated road is open most of the time and will take us down the mountain to Interstate 8. If the gate's closed, just continue on Sunrise Highway to I-8.

**T**he next five miles on Kitchen Creek Road are more dirt and potholes, but the view is spectacular. Trees leave us after a short time, revealing Southern California's standard coastal sage scrub, hugging low to the rugged terrain.

The pavement picks up near the bottom and is surprisingly nice... a smooth, lined highway that takes you from nowhere to the freeway.

Then again, why not bypass the freeway... continue under the span and make a right at Old Highway 80, another stretch of the route we took through Guatay. Watch for the hang gliders landing near Boulder Oaks. It's an easy drive to the bottom of Sunrise Highway, where you'll cross Interstate 8 into Pine Valley.

I never miss a stop in Pine Valley. In the summer, its location and towering pines always make it seem cool and comfortable. In the winter, the smoke from fireplaces seems to hang there, giving it a toasty, cozy feeling.

Of course, the ice cream at Frosty Burger could be an attraction.

From Pine Valley, follow the signs to return to I- 8.

East County's mountain communities and the Cleveland National Forest are places of contrast and rugged roads.

DRIVE
8

To really explore them, take a few days for this drive, stopping at bed and breakfasts, cabins or camping along the way.

Or, take a day and mark spots for a return. However quickly or slowly you explore, do make the journey.

## For More Information

### Restaurants/Stores/Lodging/Shopping

- **Viejas Indian Reservation, Casino and Outlet Center,** 5000 Willows Road, Alpine, (800) 84-POKER, *www.viejas.com.* Full-service casino and outlet center just east of Alpine. Several restaurants on-site.
- **Descanso Junction Cafe**, 8306 Highway 79, Descanso, (619) 445-4104. Roadside cafe open daily at junction of SR-79 and Riverside Drive.
- **Descanso Deli & Grill,** 24680 Viejas Blvd., Descanso, (619) 445-3804. Quick food in "downtown" Descanso. Next to store, post office.
- **Frosty Burger,** 28823 Old Highway 80, Pine Valley, (619) 473-9952. Drive-in restaurant with burgers and ice cream treats.
- **Major's Diner,** 28870 Old Highway 80, Pine Valley, (619) 473-9969. Old-fashioned diner includes counter seating; is a car-club favorite.
- **Pine Valley House,** 28841 Old Highway 80, Pine Valley, (619) 473-8708. Sit-down restaurant has daily specials.

Rugged Kitchen Creek Road descends quickly.

- **Mt. Laguna Lodge and Store**, 10678 Sunrise Highway, Mt. Laguna, (619) 445-2342 or (619) 473-8533, *www.lagunamountain.com*. Cabins and motel units have been a backcountry favorite since the 1920s. Store is the only place around for munchies and liquids.

### Parks and Other Attractions

- **Tryyn Galley** spoon art, 27540 Old Highway 80, Guatay, (619) 473-9030, *www.tryyn.sandiego411.net*. Gallery operated by artist Bill Chappelow, who creates jewelry and other art.

- **Cleveland National Forest:** Descanso Ranger District, 3348 Alpine Blvd., Alpine, (619) 445-6235, www.fs.fed.us/r5/cleveland/ Check here for road closures and purchase a National Forest Adventurepass.

- **Pine Valley County Park**, 28810 Old Highway 80, Pine Valley. For reservations, call (858) 565-3600. *www.sdcounty.ca.gov/parks*. This 17-acre park includes three picnic areas, a large lawn area (reservations accepted) and stands of oaks and pines. Playgrounds, horseshoes, shuffleboard, ball fields, and tennis courts are also included.

**Longtime favorite Frosty Burger in Pine Valley.**

## Drive 9

# Trail to the Stars

### Native Americans, an Escaped Slave, Star Charting, and Casinos on Pala Road

**O**ur civilization's road to discovery has taken many forms and today's unique drive through North County has four major mileposts along its 62 miles.

Before the arrival of Europeans, Native Americans lived in these valleys and hills. The 18th century brought the Spanish soldiers and Franciscan friars. In the 19th century, a runaway slave staked out his claim on a rugged mountain. And in the 20th century, a giant observatory was established to give a better view of the stars.

*Distance*

- 62 miles from start at I-15 and SR-76.
- Nate Harrison Grade is a dirt road.
- Optional side trips to Valley Center attractions.

DRIVE 9

**Pala Mission has been welcoming worshipers since 1816.**

All these landmarks are along Pala Road — SR-76 — running from Interstate 15 inland to Palomar Mountain. Along the way is one the best preserved missions, a wilderness park, and a dirt road up a steep grade to the Palomar Observatory, one of the world's largest. We'll end with a visit to a contemporary Indian casino.

Take I-15 to the Pala Road exit (SR-76), heading east. First up on the right is Casino Pala, but I suggest you visit later as the restaurants offer great choices for an end-of-day meal.

Do look for the left onto Pala Mission Road, just across from the casino entrance. After turning, watch for the mission up ahead on the left.

**M**ission San Antonio de Pala boasts that it is the only one of the original Spanish missions that continues to serve the Native American community, the Pala Indians. The town and mission are located on their reservation.

Opened in 1816 as an annex, or assistencia, to Mission San Luis Rey in Oceanside, the mission's isolated location

*For Kids And Adults*

- Kids will love the nature hikes at Wilderness Gardens, exploring the old mission at Pala, the Palomar Observatory.

- Adults might enjoy the casinos — there are four in this area.

- There's enough here to take one trip for the family, one for just mom and dad.

largely protected it from the decay that devastated most of the missions.

The original buildings, courtyard, and cemetery are well worth the visit, offering a quiet look back at the style of California's initial European settlements.

Back on eastbound SR-76 is the Wilderness Gardens County Park, which sits in the lovely San Luis Rey River valley just east of Pala.

There's a small picnic area next to the parking lot, while hiking trails fan out from the area offering wonderful views. During droughts, the riverbed is dry and the area completely brown. However, its isolation

*On The Road*

- SUVs will love Nate Harrison Grade. Four-wheel-drive or all-wheel-drive isn't really needed (it is more pleasant), but the high ground clearance can come in handy on rocky roads.

- On another day, take the sports car or motorcycle, using South Grade Road instead of Nate Harrison. The twists are a lot of fun.

provides visitors one of those rare spots to enjoy what Southern California was like before we all developed it.

Continuing east on SR-76 after a few twists and turns, we're in the fertile Pauma Valley. One of the county's agricultural centers, the fragrant orange groves and vegetable fields pump millions of dollars into the local economy.

In the midst of an orange tree forest, watch for the left turn to Nate

**Shady oaks cover Wilderness Gardens trail.**

**Rugged Nate Harrison Grade climbs quickly above Pauma Valley.**

Harrison Grade. A mile or so of pavement gives way to a graded dirt road that rises more than 4,000 feet to Palomar Mountain State Park.

One note on the weather: Palomar Mountain gets snow in the winter, sometimes heavier rains anytime of the year and extreme heat in the summer. Be prepared for anything, as it might be sunny in the valley but snow chains are required on the mountain; call the state park ranger for information.

## Rubbernecker Special

- Plenty of things to see around every turn.
- Valley and mountain views are spectacular.
- Fields and groves surrounded by mountains are unique to this area.
- Forest on Palomar Mountain has traditional look.

**N**ate Harrison was an escaped slave who settled on the mountain in the 1860s and reportedly lived a solitary life until he found out the Civil War was over — a few years after the fact. Until his death in 1920, he was well known to local settlers. Today, Harrison's 60-acre homestead is still in private hands; the road makes one of its many hairpin turns in front of one man's historic, wooded escape. A rock monument marks the spot; its bronze plaque long since disappeared.

## Directions

- I-15 to Pala Road exit, then east on Pala Road (SR-76).
- Right at Wilderness Gardens County Park.
- Left at Nate Harrison Grade (dirt road starts about a mile from SR-76 and runs for about six miles). Paved alternate: continue on SR-76 and left at South Grade Road.
- Left at Canfield Road (S-6) to Palomar Observatory.
- Leave Observatory on Canfield Road, continuing onto South Grade Road.
- Right at Pala Road (SR-76).
- Right at Pala Mission Road to Pala Mission. Continue on Pala Mission Road to Pala Casino.
- Left at Pala Road from Pala Casino.
- Continue to Interstate 15.

Allow a couple of hours for the drive up the hill. There are several wide spots in the road suitable for parking and spectacular photo opportunities. Traffic is sparse, but be vigilant; it's not only a local thoroughfare, but a favorite for bikers of both the motorized and pedal variety.

As you're driving up, imagine back to the 1930s and 1940s and the trucks hauling materials up this road for the construction of the Palomar Observatory. Although the South Grade was built to haul up the 200-inch mirror, all the other materials came via Nate Harrison Grade.

DRIVE
9

**Nate Harrison Grade ascends to conifer canopy.**

By the way, if you don't want to take the dirt road, continue on SR-76 to South Grade Road, one of two paved routes.

**A**t the top of Nate Harrison Grade, you're in the Palomar Mountain State Park. Above the timber line, the 1,897-acre park offers hiking, camping, and picnicking in a beautiful conifer forest. Pay fees at the park entry, which is at the east end of the grade (you enter at the west side of the park).

The state park is nearly surrounded by the Cleveland National Forest, which also surrounds the Observatory grounds.

*Nearby Sites*

Valley Center, just up Valley Center Road from today's route, has many sites to visit. These include:

- **Two More Casinos:** Harrah's Rincon and the Valley View are south on Valley Center Road.

- **Bell Gardens Farm:** Demonstration farm is great for kids with a picnic area, farming exhibits, a miniature train ride and lots of area to run around. Off Cole Grade Road.

- **Bates Nut Farm:** On Woods Valley Road, the farm includes picnic areas, a large shop selling all kinds of nuts, candies and other goodies, an antique store, and old town exhibit.

- **Lake Wohlford:** Recreational lake offers a wide variety of activities. Adjacent Lake Wohlfort Resort has roadhouse-style restaurant, cabins.

See "For More Information" section for addresses, Web sites.

Parked cars need to display the proper pass or fee receipt when on park or national forest lands.

Heading north on Canfield Road, drivers get their first view of the Caltech-operated Palomar Observatory, home to the 200-inch Hale Telescope. A marvel when it opened in the 1948, it is still one of the largest in the world.

The giant dome is open from 9 a.m. to 4 p.m. daily. From the viewing area at 5,500 feet above sea level, visitors can see the telescope named for George Ellery Hale, the

**Canfield Road has an Alpine look.**

Caltech astronomer who spearheaded the facility's construction.

Exhibits tell how the telescope was built, how it works, some of the discoveries it has produced and a bit on the upgrades made through the years.

Down the hill is a gift shop (open only on weekends except during the summer) and photos taken from the telescope. A video (apparently produced in the late 1970s) explains how it all works.

There are three other telescopes on the mountain: the 48-inch Oschin, the 18-inch Schmidt, and the 60-inch reflecting. Astronomers from Caltech and Cornell universities, the Carnegie Institute of Washington, and Pasadena's Jet Propulsion Laboratory use the facilities.

Headed back down the Highway to the Stars (South Grade) are several more view points to enjoy the Pauma Valley. This road was

**Giant dome covers 200-inch telescope.**

built to haul up the telescope's mirror, which couldn't survive the bumpy, dirt Nate Harrison Grade.

Westbound SR-76 will take you back to I-15. Signs point to other casinos along the way, but we're headed to Casino Pala for dinner. Built along the San Luis Rey River just five miles east of I-15, the food court has a back patio with a great view of a lake and the rolling hills.

The human drive for exploration is uniquely captured in this drive. From Native Americans living peacefully along the San Luis Rey River, through Franciscan friars and Spaniard soldiers opening up California to European settlers, to an escaped slave looking for a better life, to scientists reaching for the stars, it's all along Pauma Valley Road. Take a day and drive through 400 years of history.

## For More Information

### Parks and Other Attractions

- **Mission San Antonio de Pala,** P.O. Box 70, Pala Mission Road, Pala. Founded by Father Antonio Peyri on June 13, 1816, the mission today continues as a Catholic Church. Gift shop and grounds open daily.

- **Wilderness Gardens Park,** Highway 76, Pala, *www.sdcounty.ca.gov/ parks* and look for "open space parks." Minimal facilities — except for hiking trails — at this open space park.

- **Palomar Observatory**, end of county Highway S-6, Palomar Mountain, (626) 395-4033 (for tours), *www.astro.caltech.edu/palomarpublic*. Self-guided tours, museum open to public from 9 a.m. to 4 p.m. daily except December 24 and 25. Gift shop open some weekends.

- **Palomar Mountain State Park,** (760) 742-3462, *www.palomar.statepark.org.* Camping and day uses at 1,897-acre state park next to national forest and private areas.

- **Cleveland National Forest**, (760) 788-0250, *www.fs.fed.us/r5/ cleveland* and look for information. Federal forest area that runs from Riverside County to near the Mexican border.

- **Palomar Mountain community information**: *www.palomar mountain.com.* Includes links to local resorts, stores, and other attractions.

- **Bell Gardens Farm**, 30841 Cole Grade Road, Valley Center, (760) 749-6297, *www.bellgardensfarm.com.* Demonstration farm is great fun for kids of all ages.

- **Lake Wohlford,** 25453 Lake Wohlford Road, Escondido, (760) 839-4346, *www.ci.escondido.ca.us/visitors/lakes/wohlford/index.html.* The City of Escondido's Lake Wohlford is open seven days a week from mid-December through the weekend after Labor Day in September.

- **Lake Wohlford Resort**, 25484 Lake Wohlford Rd., Escondido. (760) 749 - 2755. RV hookups, camping, swimming pool, and cafe.

- **Bates Nut Farm**, 15954 Woods Valley Road, Valley Center, (760) 749-3333 or (800) 642-0348, *www.batesnutfarm.biz.* Since 1921, the Bates family has been farming here. The original nut stand has grown into an attraction, with a petting zoo and picnic areas in addition to a 5,000 square feet devoted to selling all kinds of nuts, candies, dried

Classic cars are a frequent sight at Bates Nut Farm in Valley Center.

**Escondido's Lake Wohlford is a mountain oasis.**

fruits, antiques, and knickknack items. Special events are held throughout the year.

### Casinos

- For detailed information on casino histories and facilities, see *Jackpot Trail: Indian Gaming In Southern California* by David Valley.

- **Pala Casino**, 11154 Highway 76, Pala, (877) 946-7252, *www.palacasino.com*. Upscale Indian casino includes a large gaming area, restaurants, hotel, and spa.

- **Pauma Casino,** 777 Pauma Reservation Road, (877) 687-2862, *www.casinopauma.com*. Modest facility with table and electronic games, and restaurant.

- **Harrah's Rincon**, 33750 Valley Center Road, Valley Center, *www.harrahs.com*. Large gaming area, restaurants, hotel, and spa at this upscale Indian casino.

- **Valley View Casino**, 16300 Nyemii Pass Road, Valley Center, (866) 843-9946, *www.valleyviewcasino.com*. Restaurant and gaming at this modest Indian casino.

  Route-O-Matic

Stuff For Kids | Required For Locals

 Great For All Vehicles

## Drive 10
# Cruisin' Old 101

### Take a Look into North Coast's Past on Historic Coast Highway

**S**an Diego County's spectacular north coast, from Oceanside to Torrey Pines, is among the most scenic spots in America. Tall cliffs and wide beaches are constant companions, marking the eastern edge of the Pacific Ocean.

For drivers who have longed for the romance of old Route 66, check out our coast highway. This was once the southern end of U.S. 101, the main road from San Diego to Los Angeles, and beyond to Canada.

After languishing for a couple of de-

### Distance

- About 30 miles from Oceanside to San Diego.

- Allow at least two hours to explore the area, plus more time to stop, eat, and shop along the way.

**Shopping at Oceanside Harbor.**

cades, the route is being revitalized from top to bottom and now sports historic highway markers, quaint restaurants, and shops. All in all, a great way to spend the day.

Until the early 1960s, this drive was the bumper-to-bumper scary ride from San Diego to Los Angeles, with parts known as "slaughter alley" for the high accident rate. Interstate 5 bypassed much of this route and 101 became a quaint, wide-open and picturesque coastal sojourn between Torrey Pines and Oceanside.

Starting in Oceanside and cruising south puts vehicles on the ocean side of the road and offers the best views through the windshield, rather than the back window. Not only is it marked with "Historic Highway U.S. 101" signs, but it's also county Highway S-21.

Going from north to south, drivers begin at Oceanside Harbor, with its miniature Seaport Village. Although a nice place to spend the day, the food is of the snack bar variety (aside from a couple of sit-down restaurants) and the shops are very touristy.

*For The Kids*

• Beaches and parks are among the best in the world.

• Fun restaurants along the way.

• If the kids misbehave, leave them at the Army-Navy Academy in Carlsbad.

Heading into Oceanside proper from the harbor, drivers cross the first of several narrow, yet original highway bridges.

Downtown Oceanside has the reputation of being primarily a liberty station from nearby Camp Pendleton, but the city fathers have worked hard over the last few years at redevelopment. There's a new multiplex movie theater, shops, and a fairly new city hall complex around the Mission

Avenue intersection.

Don't miss the California Surf Museum and a long row of classic 1940s and 1950s buildings that were once automobile show-rooms. There's even an old Kinney Shoes location that's now a beauty college. Also, check out the Oceanside Pier, park, and nearby Roberts Cottages (1920s beach houses) at the end of Mission Avenue.

Before heading into Carlsbad, you'll pass the first of four lagoons along the way. The Buena Vista Audubon Society op-erates a nature center at the south edge of Oceanside, on Buena Vista lagoon.

*Required For Locals*

A quiz:
- Where's Swami's?
- Where did Carlsbad get its name?
- Where can you get coffee in a restored railroad station?

Up the hill into Carlsbad, the old highway crosses the onetime Santa Fe railroad tracks. They swing inland for awhile but will re-join the highway in south Carlsbad.

Now Carlsbad Boulevard, the road runs through the middle of the Army-Navy Academy. Next is Magee Park, home to the Magee House and other historic structures dating from the community's founding in 1887.

The two blocks from Magee Park to Carlsbad Village Drive in-clude other sites dating to the town's founding. The Alt Karlsbad spa continues on the site where onetime sea captain John Frazier struck mineral water.

The water resembled that from a spring in Karlsbad, Poland. Carlsbad became the name of the town.

Neiman's Restaurant, the next block down, serves great food where the famous Twin Inns was located. The Victorian building

**Pier and beach at Oceanside.**

**Oceanside cafe captures the spirit of the road.**

was originally a home and later a restaurant that served chicken dinners.

Continuing south, Old 101 swings bluff-side again and past the Encina power plant. South of Poinsettia Lane is a stretch that was one of the last abandoned as the main highway.

Through an area once known as Ponto and by the South Carlsbad State Beach, look for remnants of two or more U.S. 101 alignments. The 1920s or 1930s bridges on one side and 1940s and 1950s bridges on the other reveal the road's archaeology.

Look under the sand dusting today's parking areas; in some spots there are remnants of the 1920s highway, which snaked closer to the bluffs than the later roads.

The rail line also moves closer to the highway around Poinsettia Drive and will stay with you the rest of the trip.

Leucadia is next on the route, now a part of the city of Encinitas. This stretch of old 101 still has many buildings that once housed roadside businesses catering to Los Angeles to San Diego travelers .

Old, rusting gas stations, some aban-

### On The Road

- An easy drive on mostly wide roads.
- Traffic can be heavy in areas.
- Be sure to let traffic pass as you slow and take in the view.
- Plenty of places to stop and gawk.

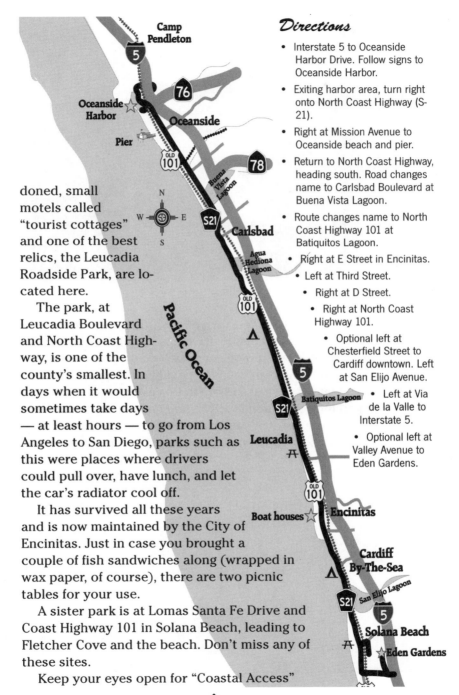

doned, small motels called "tourist cottages" and one of the best relics, the Leucadia Roadside Park, are located here.

The park, at Leucadia Boulevard and North Coast Highway, is one of the county's smallest. In days when it would sometimes take days — at least hours — to go from Los Angeles to San Diego, parks such as this were places where drivers could pull over, have lunch, and let the car's radiator cool off.

It has survived all these years and is now maintained by the City of Encinitas. Just in case you brought a couple of fish sandwiches along (wrapped in wax paper, of course), there are two picnic tables for your use.

A sister park is at Lomas Santa Fe Drive and Coast Highway 101 in Solana Beach, leading to Fletcher Cove and the beach. Don't miss any of these sites.

Keep your eyes open for "Coastal Access"

## *Directions*

- Interstate 5 to Oceanside Harbor Drive. Follow signs to Oceanside Harbor.
- Exiting harbor area, turn right onto North Coast Highway (S-21).
- Right at Mission Avenue to Oceanside beach and pier.
- Return to North Coast Highway, heading south. Road changes name to Carlsbad Boulevard at Buena Vista Lagoon.
- Route changes name to North Coast Highway 101 at Batiquitos Lagoon.
- Right at E Street in Encinitas.
- Left at Third Street.
- Right at D Street.
- Right at North Coast Highway 101.
- Optional left at Chesterfield Street to Cardiff downtown. Left at San Elijo Avenue.
- Left at Via de la Valle to Interstate 5.
- Optional left at Valley Avenue to Eden Gardens.

**Alt Karlsbad Spa dates to town's founding.**

signs along the way, or just take a turn off Old 101 toward the beach and explore. Leucadia and Encinitas have beautiful beaches at the bottom of cliffs, or at access points such as Moonlight State Beach.

Another relic along the highway is the old Encinitas train station, now a Pannikin coffee house at 510 North Coast Highway 101 in Leucadia. Slated for demolition in 1975, the Encinitas 101 web site reports that Carlsbad resident Jim Bowen and architect John Henderson moved the station north to Leucadia and restored it. It's

**South Carlsbad State Beach.**

DRIVE
10

a wonderful example of a pre-101 structure.

Downtown Encinitas really been spruced up in recent years, with new sidewalks, street lights and, in front of the La Paloma Theater, an overhead neon sign in the spirit of a similar sign from the 1920s.

The La Paloma itself is a living jewel, still showing movies and remaining the heart of the coastal neighborhood. Encinitas itself has more of its population living east of Interstate 5, but the coastal strip has retained its funky character. Explore the shops and restaurants from Encinitas south to the Self Realization Fellowship.

Take a side trip off Old 101 to 726-732 Third Street and see a pair of unique homes, the Boat Houses, built by Miles Kellogg in 1929. Remember, they're private homes and not open for tours. The story is that Kellogg used salvaged wood from an old Encinitas dance hall; the low ceilings inspired him to create the boats.

### *Camping*

- Beach camping is available at South Carlsbad State Beach and San Elijo State Beach.

- The experience of sleeping next to the ocean is unique.

- So is the noise from the trains running all day and night.

- See "For More Information" section in this chapter for web sites and telephone numbers for these campgrounds.

Continuing south, the gold onion-dome of the Self Realization Fellowship is the unofficial dividing line between Encinitas and Cardiff-By-The-Sea. The center was opened by Paramahansa Yogananda in Encinitas in 1937. The nearby beach is called "Swami's" as a back-

**Old U.S. 101 alignments are today's southbound lanes and parking.**

**Tiny Leucadia Roadside Park is a relic from past.**

handed tribute to the Fellowship.

Cardiff's downtown is on the east side of the railroad tracks. You'll have to make a left at Chesterfield Drive to visit. If you need a snack at this point, stop in at V.G. Donuts, 106 Aberdeen. The Mettee family has been serving up donuts and other goodies here for more than 30 years.

San Elijo State Beach offers blufftop camping and day uses. It's one of the most popular spots in the region for sleeping next to the surf.

Cardiff's Restaurant Row is just south on Old Highway 101. A collection of surf- and lagoon-side restaurants — some upscale — draw patrons from all over the county.

After passing through the San Elijo Lagoon, it's up on top of the

**Old Encinitas train depot is Leucadia coffee house.**

bluffs again to Solana Beach. Go east on Lomas Santa Fe to Cedros Street for what is arguably the premier interior design and art district in the county.

From here, continue south on Old 101 to Via de la Valle, making a left

**La Paloma Theater building in downtown Encinitas.**

at the Del Mar Fairgrounds. Off the coast, we're heading to our last stop, Eden Gardens, for some of the best Mexican food in the county. This small *colonia* with restaurants such as Fidel's and Tony's Jacal, is one of the oldest Latino communities in North County.

**Landlocked boat houses in Encinitas.**

The preservation of Old 101 is a testimonial to the hard work of the local residents, who, despite development pressures, have kept intact its character. The people who originally built the coast highway would be proud.

## For More Information

- **Oceanside Harbor Village**, Oceanside Harbor Drive, *www.nvo.com/ oceanside/oceansideharbor/* Quaint, Seaport Village-style attraction.
- **Helgren's Sportfishing**, 315 Harbor Drive South, Oceanside, (760) 722-2133, *www.helgrensportfishing.com* Sea trips from Oceanside harbor.
- **Buena Vista Audubon Society Nature Center**, 2202 South Coast Highway, Oceanside, (760) 439-BIRD, *www.bvaudubon.org* Hidden na-

**Cedros Street marker echos Quonset huts that house many businesses.**

ture center on south edge of Oceanside.

- **Carlsbad History**, City of Carlsbad online historic tour, *www.carlsbad.ca.us/historic.html* Walking, driving tour opens up beachfront town.

- **Alt Karlsbad Spa**, 2802 Carlsbad Blvd., Carlsbad, (760) 434-1887, *www.carlsbadmineralspa.com* Historic mineral spa continues distributing water from blufftop spring.

- **South Carlsbad State Beach**, Carlsbad Boulevard, (760) 438-3143, *www.parks.ca.gov*. Long beach is rocky in spots.

- **Encinitas** history tour from the Encinitas Main Street Association, *www.encinitas101.com/drive101.htm* History comes alive in growing beach town.

- **Self-Realization Fellowship**, 215 K Street, Encinitas, (760) 753-2888. Cliffside religious center.

- **V.G. Donuts**, 106 Aberdeen, Cardiff, (760) 753-2400, *www.vgbakery.com* Goodies at local favorite make a nice road snack.

- **San Elijo State Beach**, Cardiff, (760) 753-5091, *www.parks.ca.gov/* Great camping spot in Cardiff-By-The-Sea.

- **Cedros Design District**, South Cedros Street, Solana Beach. *www.cedrosdesigndistrict.com* Attracts designers and consumers from all over Southern California.

- **Fidel's Restaurant**, 607 Valley Avenue, Eden Gardens, Solana Beach, (858) 755-5292. Historic Eden Gardens restaurant, just north of Del Mar Racetrack.

- **Tony's Jacal Restaurant**, 621 Valley Avenue), Eden Gardens, Solana Beach, (858) 755-2274. Another historic Eden Gardens restaurant.

DRIVE 10

## Section 3

# South Bay and South-of-the-Border

### Tijuana River Valley, Otay, Baja California

**H**ey, here's a secret... some of the best drives in South ern California aren't in the mountains to the east or north, or in the desert.

Some of them are right around the corner, if you live in San Diego's South Bay area.

A couple more are just across the border in Mexico.

Here are five drives that might surprise even veteran San Diego area cruisers: the Tijuana River Valley around and through Imperial Beach; the Olympic Training Center, Otay Lakes Road, and beyond; the Otay Mountain Wilderness; the toll road between Tijuana and Ensenada; and Baja's Highway 3 between El Sauzal and Tecate.

As I discuss in Chapter 11, I have friends — natives to San Diego's South Bay — who have never explored the Tijuana River Estuary. This is one of the largest remaining wetlands in Southern California and offers a lot for drivers and horseback riders.

The Olympic Training Center, next to the Lower Otay Reservoir, is unfortunately one of San Diego's best kept secrets. Athletes from around the country train at this facility year-round, and it depends on locals for support. Beyond are some great roads.

And who's heard of the Otay Mountain Wilderness area? Not even its neighbors in Dulzura and at the South Bay Rod and Gun Club, which sits in its shadow. This is a fabulous, isolated drive through an unspoiled preserve.

South of the border, most folks know about the toll road from Tijuana to Ensenada; few have taken it. It is one of the most spectacular drives anywhere, as it rides on cliffs overlooking the Pacific Ocean. Northern California's Highway 1 offers similar terrain, but the arid Baja climate gives a completely different look.

And from the blank stares I get, most of my gringo friends have never even thought of driving from Ensenada (actually just north at El Sauzal) to Tecate. Highway 3 winds through beautiful valleys and rugged hills... and a lot of history.

If you miss South Bay and Baja, you've missed a lot. So fill up the gas tank and head out for some very surprising cruises.

## *Drive 11*

# Valley of Contrasts

### *The Tijuana River Estuary and Imperial Beach, Silver Strand and Coronado*

**P**erhaps no place on earth better illustrates two meanings of the word "bluff."

Physically, it is a bluff — a high, steep bank — on the edge of the Pacific Ocean, at the most southwesterly point of the continental United States.

The peacefulness is also a bluff — a deception. On one hand, a typically sunny Southern California afternoon beckons visitors with roar of the surf, the cry of the sea gulls, the Pacific coast vista — seemingly endless to the north, and a sleepy village and bullfighting ring to

### *Distance*

- About 30 Miles
- Easy access from Interstate 5 in San Ysidro.
- Dirt road to Border Field State Park usually OK for cars but may require SUV – if it's open at all.

**View from Border Field State Park.**

the south. A park — Border Field State Park — green lawn, picnic tables, barbecues, children playing.

Now, here's the deception: the fence. It snakes out of the hills and into the surf. This is the border between the United States and Mexico. Border Patrol officers are on duty.

At night, it's brightly lit and more U.S. officers cruise the hills in sport-utility vehicles, a battle zone within sight of downtown Tijuana. San Diego's skyscrapers light up the horizon.

But we're visiting during the day, when the Tijuana River Valley can be enjoyed as a remarkable preserve in the middle of two great international cities.

Over the years this area has been a Naval bombing range and was envisioned as a marina.

It has a reputation as a place where sewage flows and international politics have made it a sometime flash point.

But the valley is still a place that can and should be enjoyed as one of the last and best preserved wetlands on the coast.

Ride a horse on the beach. Look up the coast and see much the same view as Native Americans enjoyed before the Spanish

### For The Kids

- Interactive exhibits at Tijuana Estuary Visitors' Center.
- Nature hikes.
- Horseback riding.
- Play area and fishing at Imperial Beach Pier.

### Caution

- Keep away from streams in estuary area.

arrived.

No condos, no freeways, except off in the distance. And all about 20 minutes from downtown San Diego, which is barely visible on a clear day.

To get there, head south on Interstate 5. Just a couple of exits before the border, look for Dairy Mart Road. Named for the long-gone Dairy Mart Dairy (which, along with others, such as Hages and Golden Arrow, used to home-deliver milk), the quick right turn after exiting Interstate 5 takes drivers almost instantly out in the country.

**Horse Friendly**

- Equestrian facilities and trails are throughout the southern part of the estuary. Public corrals are at the Border Field State Park entry and at the county's Tijuana River Valley Regional Park ranger station on Hollister Street.

- Sandy's Rental Stables offers rental horses and trail guides on Hollister Street.

**T**he river quickly makes its presence known, as a fairly new bridge takes Dairy Mart Road south. On the left, a sod farm and a model airplane field let you know you're not in the city any more, although straight ahead, on the other side of the fence, traffic buzzes on Baja's Highway 1. Reeds and coastal sage scrub mark the Tijuana River.

As Dairy Mart Road curves, it changes to Monument Road, honoring the U.S.-Mexico border marker at the park.

The road curves gently around the south bluff of the river's gorge. Quickly, you'll notice the first of many stables. Hundreds of horses are boarded and bred in the valley.

**Looking south is the border and Tijuana's Playas neighborhood.**

**Hollister Street is a pleasant drive.**

Continue down Monument Road, such as it is, past Hollister Street. Bumpy, pitted when paved, rocky and potholed when dirt, it is passable. It is not passable after a heavy rain, so if the road is a pond, come back another day. Here's an opportunity for those with SUVs to actually drive off the pavement, but I've got a two-seat sports car and took it with no problem. Just keep your eyes open and slow down.

Driving north, the farms end and the preserve begins. All told, the combined Tijuana River Valley Regional Park, part Tijuana River National Estuarine Sanctuary, Border Field State Park and Tijuana Slough National Wildlife Refuge cover 2,500 acres. One of 23 estuarine reserves in the country devoted to education and research, it is a place to bird watch, hike, horseback ride, and enjoy the coast of our ancestors.

**P**ast the park entrance, the road curves south to the Border Field State Park, up on our bluff. After driving for a few miles through the middle of nowhere, it seems a bit surprising to turn into a parking lot for a very conventional park — picnic tables, barbecues.

To the north is the reserve, the west the ocean, the south Tijuana's saucer-shaped Bullring by the Sea and adjacent neighborhood, and to the east the mountains and South Bay cities.

Farther north, the skyscrapers of downtown San Diego can be seen on a clear day. Beyond, Point Loma rises Gibralter-like out of the sea.

Take some time to enjoy the view and check out The Monument — one of a chain that stretches to the Gulf Coast of Texas marking the border between the United States and Mexico. Look at the border fence. Talk with the friendly Border Patrol agents. And chat

## Directions

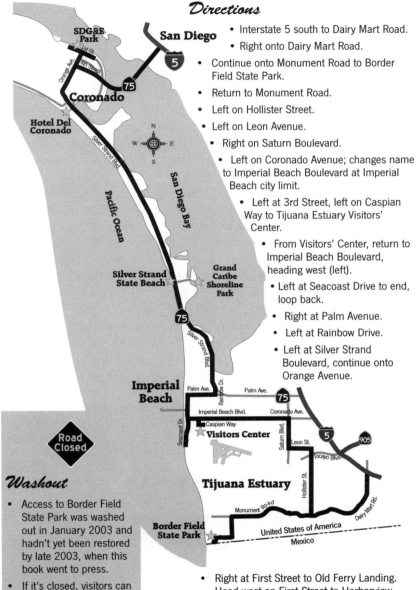

- Interstate 5 south to Dairy Mart Road.
- Right onto Dairy Mart Road.
- Continue onto Monument Road to Border Field State Park.
- Return to Monument Road.
- Left on Hollister Street.
- Left on Leon Avenue.
- Right on Saturn Boulevard.
- Left on Coronado Avenue; changes name to Imperial Beach Boulevard at Imperial Beach city limit.
- Left at 3rd Street, left on Caspian Way to Tijuana Estuary Visitors' Center.
- From Visitors' Center, return to Imperial Beach Boulevard, heading west (left).
- Left at Seacoast Drive to end, loop back.
- Right at Palm Avenue.
- Left at Rainbow Drive.
- Left at Silver Strand Boulevard, continue onto Orange Avenue.

## Washout

- Access to Border Field State Park was washed out in January 2003 and hadn't yet been restored by late 2003, when this book went to press.
- If it's closed, visitors can reach the beach by parking by the "Road Closed" sign.
- Walk the half-mile to the ocean.

- Right at First Street to Old Ferry Landing. Head west on First Street to Harborview (SDG&E) Park.
- Return to Orange Avenue.
- Left at 4th Street to San Diego-Coronado Bay Bridge and I-5.

## On The Road

- Mostly an easy drive on paved roads.

- Entry to Border Field State Park can be muddy or sandy, depending on the time of year. Access can be closed during rainy season. Vehicles with high ground clearance may be needed.

- Once at Border Field State Park, there's a large, nicely paved parking lot. Go figure.

with the folks on the other side of the border through the mesh fence.

The view is spectacular. A wide, sandy beach is a short hike down the hill. And, if the water is clean, it's OK to swim.

Heading back, retrace your route to Hollister Street and turn left. Stables rent horses for the day; one even has guided tours to the beach. Riding there, I'm told, is a unique experience for both horse and rider.

Continuing north, you're in the City of San Diego community of Nestor, which lies between the City of Imperial Beach and Interstate 5. It's hard to see, but you're circling one of the lesser known Naval bases in San Diego, the Imperial Beach Naval Auxiliary Landing Field, also known as Ream Field.

We've now driven around the preserve and are about to learn about it. The Estuary Visitors' Center is just off Imperial Beach Boulevard. Follow the signs and turn left at 3rd Street and around to the center. Open daily, the center offers exhibits on the flora and fauna

**Estuary and visitors' center at Imperial Beach.**

**Sunny day on Imperial Beach Pier.**

in the estuary, as well as a fabulous view of the marsh.

Friendly park service employees point out sites and birds, and paths lead away from the center. Staff and an active volunteer program provide nature walks and bird walks on weekends, a speaker series on Friday and for kids a Junior Rangers program on Thursday afternoons.

**T**he estuary is home to endangered species such as the California Least Tern and American Peregrine Falcon. Bring your binoculars. Estuaries like Tijuana used to be located every few miles along the coast — almost every place where a river met the sea. However, most have been developed, leaving few places for migrating birds and other wildlife.

The last view we'll have of the estuary on today's drive is from across the slough, on Imperial Beach's Seacoast Drive. Condos line the beach, but the view of the estuary is open. Parking is available so take advantage of the opportunity to hike both the beach and estuary.

Do spend some time in Imperial Beach, a funky beach town that hasn't been too gentrified — the rough edges make it interesting. The pier and adjacent park have recently been spruced up, and while there are a few new shops, this is IB. If you're looking for Seaport Village, you won't find it here.

Continue on to Coronado on the Silver Strand, a skinny strip of

**Bike path on Silver Strand.**

land that separates the bay from the ocean. There's more traffic these days (like everywhere else), but taking the Strand lets you see some more open space in the middle of San Diego. The county's Ecological Research area is just north of the old salt ponds (extracted salt is used for water purification and other industrial processes). The paved bicycle path (on the old railroad right-of-way) and the Coronado Cays development (exclusive waterfront homes) are along the way.

The Silver Strand State Beach is one of the nicest ones (day use, $4) and one of the few places with RV parking right on the beach.

Coronado is next. This beach town, which starts with the Hotel Del Coronado and Coronado Shores towers, is worth a day to explore.

We can't cover here, but if you continue through town to the end of Orange Avenue, there's a bit of San Diego transportation history. One of the old ticket booths is all that's left of the San Diego--Coronado car ferry, which quit in 1969 when the bridge opened. To the south is the Old Ferry Landing development, a collection of shops and restaurants.

From here, it's just a few blocks back to 4th Street and over the bridge to San Diego.

Today's drive has visited several spots of nearly unspoiled beauty, harkening back to the days before San Diego and Tijuana became a megalopolis. We've wound our way from the controversial border and up the coast to the lovely seaside community of Coronado. Hope you didn't forget your binoculars and camera.

Silver Strand State Beach.

## For More Information

**Tijuana Estuary Parks**

- **Border Field State Park,** west end of Monument Road, (619) 575-3613, open daily 9:30 a.m. to 5 p.m., however the access road may be closed due to weather conditions. *www.parks.ca.gov* and search for park.

- **Tijuana River Valley County Park**, Hollister Street, (858) 694-3049 *www.co.san-diego.ca.us* and search for park.

- **Tijuana Estuary Visitors' Center**, 301 Caspian Way, (619) 575-2704, open daily 10 a.m. to 5 p.m. *www.parks.ca.gov* and search for park.

Old Coronado Ferry toll booth at Ferry Landing Park in Coronado.

**View of downtown San Diego from Harborview (SDG&E) Park, Coronado.**

- **Tijuana River National Estuarine Research Reserve**, information from the federal perspective. *www.tijuanaestuary.com* and *www.ocrm.nos.noaa.gov* and search for Tijuana River.

### Other Parks

- **Silver Strand State Beach**, Silver Strand Boulevard/California 75 at Silver Strand State Beach exit, (619) 435-5184.

### Rent-A-Horse

- **Sandy's Rental Stable**, 5060 Hollister Street, (619) 424-3124. *www.sandysrentalstable.com* Rent horses for rides to the beach. Organized activities available as well.

### Restaurants/Shops

- **Beach Club Grille**, 710 Seacoast Drive, Imperial Beach, (619) 628-0777, *www.beachclubgrille.com*. Friendly local cafe open on weekends for breakfast, seven days a week for lunch, dinner.

- **Tin Fish** at the Imperial Beach Pier, Seacoast Drive, Imperial Beach, (619) 628-8414. Seafood fast-food cafe, beer and wine, at end of pier.

- **Bibbey's Seashell Shop,** 903 Seacoast Drive, (619) 423-5133 *www.ib-chamber.org/BibbeysShells.htm* Classic seaside gift shop.

### Cities, Etc.

- **City of Imperial Beach**, official Web site, *www.cityofib.com*
- **City of Coronado,** official Web site, *www.coronado.ca.us*
- **San Diego Bay,** San Diego Unified Port District bay tourism site, *www.thebigbay.com*

## Drive 12

# Olympians & Horses

### Twisting Through Otay Lakes, Olympians, Honey Springs, Lyons Valley, and Jamul

**T**he rolling hills of southern San Diego county were once home to some of the largest cattle ranches in Southern California, with thousands of head roaming Otay Ranch, Rancho Jamul, and other spreads just north of the Mexican border.

Today, these agricultural lands are quickly becoming home to new herds that feed at McDonald's instead of on the lush grasses — subdivisions are growing like weeds in this area.

This drive goes through what's left of these ranches plus some areas that are likely to be preserved for future generations. It will

### Distance

- About 45 miles.
- Plan a couple of hours at the ARCO Olympic Training Center.

**Olympic Training Center entry.**

also traverse one of the "crookedest" roads in the county and over its approximately 45 miles go from civilization to the middle of nowhere and back to civilization — from Chula Vista, through Otay to Jamul through the county's southeastern mountains.

From Interstate 805, slice east through a quick six miles of new developments along Olympic Parkway. Watch for signs pointing to the ARCO Olympic Training Center.

The road climbs gently from I-805 to our first destination, the ARCO Olympic Training Center.

The center is worth visiting. Home to many of America's Olympic hopefuls, the training center has a nifty gift shop, guided and self-guided tours, and a movie on the center and America's Olympic movement.

On the guided tour, the knowledgeable docents provide lots of trivia about this still-developing center. Wear walking shoes as it's more than a mile walk around the complex.

There are lots of places to picnic, with both tables and wide lawns, but bring your own because there is no public food ser-

*For The Kids*

- U.S. Olympic Training Center is unique.
- See cattle and horses up close... if they're grazing close to the road.
- Twisting roads can be a thrill.

vice at the center, only soda machines.

The Lower Otay Reservoir offers a rustic park under fragrant eucalyptus trees, open for picnicking and fishing on Wednesdays, Saturdays, and Sundays. There is no charge for using the park, but anglers need to get a fishing license at the tiny store. Boats are for rent; no swimming, though.

### On The Road

- Good for any vehicle as route is all paved.

- Traffic lessens after passing the Otay lakes.

- Hairpin turns on Honey Springs Road and Lyons Valley Road are lots of fun or nerve-wracking, depending on your point of view.

- Take Skyline Truck Trail at the intersection with Lyons Valley Road and Honey Spring Road for a less-twisty route.

**O**ne of the oldest serving the city of San Diego's water system (yes, you might be drinking water from this lake), Lower Otay's dam broke in the great flood of 1916 (some say this was the basis of the play and movie, "The Rainmaker"). From the park area you can see the top of the dam, but there's no paved road that offers a view of the front.

Head north on Wueste Road, then east on Otay Lakes Road, hugging the shore of the lake. At the first sharp curve on Otay Lakes Road, take a quick

**Spartan facilities at Lower Otay Reservoir.**

**U.S. team flags fly around courtyard at Olympic Training Center.**

glance to the left and you'll see the dam of the Upper Otay Reservoir, while up further, cattle forage on the craggy hills.

A facility on the east end of the lake offers skydiving, for those of you wanting to get a better view.

The first real twisty section of Otay Lakes Road is ahead. In addition to curves, the road also goes up and down through gorges and streams with names like Dulzura Creek, Cedar Creek, and Little Cedar Creek. This is a hot, arid area, with hills covered by generally tinder-dry coastal sage scrub; the fire hazard can be extreme.

Valleys are filled with native oaks, giving a cool respite. At mile 15 is the Thousand Trails Resort Pio Pico, offering campsites and a

**Otay Lakes Road runs through beautiful valley.**

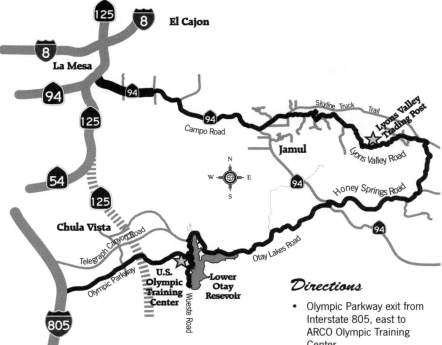

little store. Load up on liquids at this point since you won't see another market for 30 miles. There are picnic tables out back.

After another three miles is SR-94. Especially on the weekends, Highway 94 is pretty busy, so be careful turning left, then a quick right, to Honey Springs Road.

You'll rock and roll north over hills, valleys, gorges, and ravines through places such as Deerhorn Valley, a collection of ranchettes on the western edge of the Cleveland National Forest. Enjoy the drive and watch the speedometer.

The next turn is a left onto Lyons Valley Road, 18 miles of narrow, twisting asphalt. This route dates to 1851 and was opened up by Army Capt. Nathaniel Lyon, who was

## *Directions*

- Olympic Parkway exit from Interstate 805, east to ARCO Olympic Training Center.

- Exit Olympic center, turning right onto Olympic Parkway.

- Right at Wueste Road to Lower Otay Reservoir park.

- Exiting reservoir, return north on Wueste Road.

- Right at Otay Lakes Road.

- Left at SR-94 (Campo Road).

- Right at Honey Springs Road.

- Left at Lyons Valley Road.

- Right at SR-94 (Campo Road).

- Left onto Jamacha Road (staying on SR-94).

- Continue onto freeway, west to Interstate 805, north on SR-125 to Interstate 8.

DRIVE 12

**Spirited driving along Honey Springs Road in Deerhorn Valley.**

looking for a faster route east to Yuma. The valley was named in his honor.

Highlights along Lyons Valley Road include an ostrich farm and the quaint Lyons Valley Trading Post (drinks and munchies only). Mostly, though, you'll be driving on the edge of cliffs as the road winds up and down the sides of this rugged valley. Watch for the merge back with Skyline Truck Trail, then head into Jamul.

One of San Diego County's horse capitals, there may be more equines than humans here. Enjoy the views of the lovely homes and the shade of the trees.

Jamul has a number of quaint restaurants and unique shops. Locals like the Greek Sombrero (yes, Greek and Mexican food), El Coyote and El Campo (Mexican), and Tatsus (Japanese), not to mention a Filippi's Pizza. Shopping includes Simpson's Garden Town Nursery (don't miss the car collection) and the Ranch Feed Store (tack and supplies), with shops running mostly from Jefferson Street to the west along SR-94 to Steele Canyon Road.

**W**hen done touring Jamul, head west on SR-94 (Campo Road) back towards San Diego. Although a busy road, SR-94 takes its time winding through the foothills. Ranchettes dot the hills, and a new high school has just been completed.

The last "country" site is the old Campo Road trestle on the left,

just before Rancho San Diego. Known as
the Sweetwater River Bridge, it was replaced a few years back but is still open to
foot traffic and bicycles.

*Horse Friendly*

- The area east of Chula
  Vista is horse country.

- Stables abound, and
  there are riding trails
  throughout Jamul.

Civilization makes its reappearance in a
big way. Commercial development in Rancho San Diego has exploded in the past few
years, so it's not so backcountry any more.
At the junction with Jamacha Road, follow
94 by making a left. A couple of miles later, you're back on the freeway.

South County is developing fast, but it still has some of the most
spectacular roads in the region. There are still unspoiled square
miles within a few minutes' drive of most of central San Diego.

## *For More Information*

- **ARCO Olympic Training Center**, 2800 Olympic Parkway, Chula Vista.
  (619) 656-1500 *www.usoc.org* and follow "Visit Us" links to the Chula
  Vista, Calif., location. The first U.S. Olympic facility built from the
  ground-up for America's world athletes, the center is home to training camps for eight sports: archery, canoe/kayak, cycling, field
  hockey, rowing, soccer, tennis, and track and field. Well stocked gift
  shop for your favorite souvenirs, picnic areas and walking trails. No
  public food service. Tours: 9 a.m. to 4 p.m. Monday-Saturday, noon
  to 5 p.m. Sunday.

**Twists mark Lyons Valley Road.**

**Sweetwater River Bridge is near Rancho San Diego.**

- **Lower Otay Reservoir:** Otay Lakes Road and Wueste Drive. *www.sandiego.gov/water/recreation/lotay.shtml.* Reservoir offers fishing and day uses. Permit required for fishing.

- **Thousand Trails Resort Pio Pico,** 14615 Otay Lakes Rd., (619) 421-2847. *www.thousandtrails.com* Membership-only campground, but visitors are welcome to spend money at the store and snack bar along Otay Lakes Road.

- **Lyons Valley Trading Post,** 17608 Lyons Valley Rd., Jamul. (619) 468-3172. *www.lyonsvalleytradingpost.com.* Country store offers cold beverages and snacks.

# Drive 13
# Close-In Oasis
## The Otay Mountain Truck Trail

**I** **guess if we're** going to have wilderness areas, they should be hard to find.

On a beautiful spring day, having secured a rented SUV, I set off to find one of the more intriguing squiggles on the map, the Otay Mountain Truck Trail, running through the Otay Mountain Wilderness Area, just north of the Mexican border and east of San Diego's Otay Mesa area.

I headed to Dulzura to find the east entrance of the trail. However, nobody there seemed to know where the road starts.

The maps show the route begins at Marron Valley Road, which

### Distance

- About 22 miles from Dulzura to Otay Mesa.

- Allow additional travel time to Dulzura, about 20 miles east of Interstate 805 and Olympic Parkway interchange, and from Otay Mesa to I-805, another five miles.

**Trail climbs quickly from Marron Valley Road junction.**

heads south from Highway 94 about a mile southeast of the Dulzura Cafe. After driving about a mile on the dirt Marron Valley Road, I stopped in at what looked like it might be the last point of civilization along the way, the South Bay Rod and Gun Club's shooting range.

No, the gents there didn't know where the Otay Mountain Truck Trail was located; in fact they said they had trouble finding the shooting range, even though they'd been driving there for years. Hope they have a better time finding the bull's-eye with a bullet.

**B**ack to the Dulzura Cafe, where the stragglers still around at its 2 p.m. closing hadn't heard of it either. However, the bartender looked at the map, guessing it was probably well past the Gun Club.

*Stuff For Kids*

• Here's a day away from the video games and TV, out in the country air.

Off I went again, back over Marron Valley Road, south through the valley, which narrows to a gorge past the Gun Club. In fact, there's a big turnaround spot down the hill from the club that makes it look like the end of Marron Valley Road. Don't be fooled, as the route goes all the way to the U.S./Mexico border, less than five miles

DRIVE
13

south.

Just over two miles from SR-94, in the shade of a natural oak grove, is a house or two and a turn with a rusty sign pointing to... the Otay Mountain Truck Trail.

**Q**uickly, **the tone** is set for the drive. The narrow, gravel road climbs about 500 feet in less than a mile as it leaves Sycamore Canyon and Marron Valley Road. And, about two miles further, a Bureau of Land Management sign — fit for a highway — notes that we've crossed into the Otay Mountain Wilderness Area, part of the Otay National Cooperative Land and Wildlife Management Area.

This is 18,500 acres of rugged mountains and steep gorges. The gravel road normally has steep slopes on both sides, either headed up or down. Fortunately, there are occasional turnouts to stop and take in the view or let another car go by.

The proximity to the border means lots of Border Patrol activity so be sure to let the officers pass. Reminders are several signs in-

**On The Road**

- A good place to exercise the SUV or all-wheel-drive wagon.
- Challenging, narrow gravel and dirt roads from the time route leaves SR-94 until Alta Road.
- Not recommended for sports cars or other vehicles with low ground clearance.
- Only room for one vehicle along most parts of the route. Pay attention to turnouts and use them.

**Wilderness offers spectacular vistas.**

### Backyard Byway

- Trail is just a few minutes drive for the hundreds of thousands of people living in San Diego's South Bay and East County communities.

- One of the best ways to view an area mostly unspoiled by man.

structing travelers, in Spanish, not to set campfires due to the severe fire danger.

The road itself is mostly gravel. A car could make it, but I'm glad I left the Miata home and opted for a Jeep Liberty. I had the part-time four-wheel-drive engaged most of the way for extra sure-footedness. Four-wheel-drive low isn't needed, but it's good exercise for those of you with all-wheel-drive systems that really never get used on San Diego's freeways.

The BLM reports that this is the largest stand of Tecate Cypress, a rare, shrub-like tree that clings to the rugged hillsides. Some are large enough to partially shade the road, but most wouldn't clear the roof of the Jeep.

There are at least 37 other rare or endangered plants in the preserve, with oak and sycamore stands in the valleys and coastal sage scrub dominating the rest of the area.

**A** wilderness area it is, but one that definitely reflects our local climate and topography. There aren't any forests here, just our native low-lying brush. Still, it is a breathtaking preserve.

This is pretty much just a drive with a few places to stop, as

**Sign marks entry to wilderness area.**

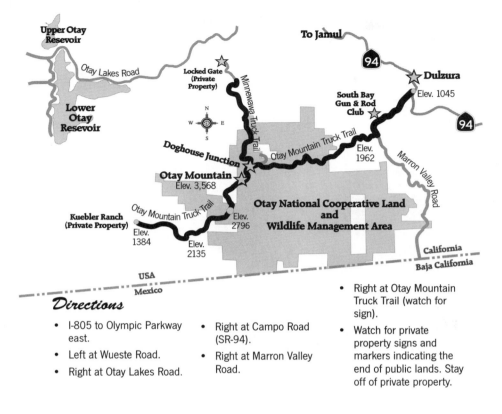

## Directions

- I-805 to Olympic Parkway east.
- Left at Wueste Road.
- Right at Otay Lakes Road.

- Right at Campo Road (SR-94).
- Right at Marron Valley Road.

- Right at Otay Mountain Truck Trail (watch for sign).
- Watch for private property signs and markers indicating the end of public lands. Stay off of private property.

there aren't any marked hiking trails in the area. Camping is allowed, but there are no campsites. The BLM advises a phone call to (760) 251-4800 in advance if you want to hike or camp.

**E**levations go above 3,500 feet over the 20 miles of the truck trail, plus another four miles if you take a side road, the Minnewawa Truck Trail, which heads north from Doghouse Junction. You can't miss Doghouse Junction because, although the doghouse is long gone, drivers find themselves at a scissors crossing, with two roads seemingly headed to antenna farms, while another goes northwest.

The Minnewawa Truck Trail (the center-right road) offers great views of the Lower Otay Reservoir and Otay Lakes Road. The problem is that the road runs into private property just before reaching Otay Lakes Road near the Thousand Trails Resort Pio Pico. The day I visited, there was a locked gate (five padlocks, no less) that pre-

**Otay lakes are visible from Minnewawa Truck Trail.**

vented me from descending. I had to back up a quarter mile before there was enough room to turn around.

So, if you do drive up Minnewawa, don't go past where the gravel road turns to rocks and ruts. There's a turn-around that you can't miss — use it.

The Otay Mountain Truck Trail continues southwest from Doghouse Junction, around the namesake mountain, elevation 3,566 and topped with several antennas. At this point, vistas to the south open up, giving views of Tijuana's eastern neighborhoods, about 3,000 feet below. You'll also see some old bunkers, remnants of artillery emplacements created before World War II.

**A**t this point, you're only about a mile from the boundary between the United States and Mexico, and the Border Patrol will make its presence known. Along the drive, I saw a half-dozen of the Patrol's SUVs parked in various wide spots, watching for folks trying to make the trek north from Mexico without going through the usual channels. The officers are friendly, one thankfully letting me know I was, in fact, on the right road.

I also met a couple of other trucks and SUVs along the way. If you can, head for a turnout, otherwise the vehicle heading down the slope is supposed to back up to the next turnout, giving the vehicle heading up the hill the right-of-way. Everybody seemed courteous and followed the rules the day I drove the trail.

A bit crazier are the mountain bikers. While headed up the

grade, driving slowly, I came upon a couple of cyclists headed downhill at a pretty good clip. I had to swerve to get out of their way, as they didn't seem interested in yielding to me. Keep your eyes open.

From Otay Mountain, the road descends about 500 feet every half-mile, curving around the peaks that are part of the San Ysidro Mountains. Views alternate between San Diego and Tijuana, giving visitors a spectacular perspective on our region. The ocean, Point Loma, and the mountains of Baja California frame the vista.

**Narrow road has room for only one vehicle.**

This is about the time to turn around and head back to Dulzura. A large sign (facing the other direction) marks the edge of the Otay Mountain Wilderness Area. Beyond, the road is in private property and not open to the public. Don't take it.

The drive was even better the second time through, as I saw things I missed the first time.

Otay Mountain is visible from much of the central and southern part of the county. I'm glad it's been preserved, and that we can take such a beautiful drive through a well preserved part of natural San Diego.

**Windshield vista is spectacular.**

Eastern Tijuana neighborhoods are a reminder civilization is returning.

## *For More Information*

- **Otay Mountain Wilderness, U.S. Bureau of Land Management:** *www.ca.blm.gov/palmsprings/otay_mtns_wilderness.html*. For information, contact the offices in North Palm Springs or Jamul: South Coast Field Office, 690 West Garnet Avenue, N. Palm Springs, (760) 251-4800.

- **Dulzura Cafe**: 16985 SR-94, Dulzura, (619) 468-9591. Classic roadhouse serving burgers, beers, and billiards. Favorite for car and motorcycle clubs. Open until 2 p.m.

- **South Bay Rod and Gun Club**, Marron Valley Road, Dulzura, (619) 299-9744, 9 a.m. to 8:30 p.m. *www.southbayrodandgunclub.org*.

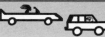

## Drive 14

# Baja's Coast Road

### The Spectacular Toll Highway from Tijuana to Ensenada

**C**alifornia's coast is a special place in the world, where rugged cliffs rise from the blue Pacific, broken up by the occasional wide beaches, coves, and bays.

That coast continues south from the arbitrary line called the U.S.-Mexico border and to miss it just because of language or other international barriers is just silly.

So, pack up the car and head south 70 miles or so to Ensenada, Baja California. Along the way, Tijuana's cosmopolitan congestion gives way to Rosarito Beach's partying, a modern movie studio, and a toll

### Distance

- About 145 miles round trip (100 km. each way).

- Allow time for stops along the way in Rosarito Beach, Ensenada.

- Or just spend the night in Ensenada and return via Tecate (see Drive 15).

DRIVE 14

**Toll plazas include rest rooms, tourist information.**

road that hugs rugged, volcanic cliffs.

Artists' colonies, delicious food, history, and fabulous vistas are your highway companions. For my trip, I also took along a copy of Greg Niemann's book, *Baja Legends*. I'll share a couple of Niemann's fascinating tidbits as we motor down the peninsula.

Head south to the border along Interstates 5 or 805. Both converge at the International Border. You'll need insurance, as most U.S. insurance is not good in Mexico. Several shops sell it adjacent to the border, so make a stop before leaving the U.S.

We're not stopping in Tijuana today, so follow the signs to Ensenada, via Mexico Highway 1-D. Markers will point to Ensenada or the "Scenic Road" — follow them as you loop around to the busy Avenida Internacíonal. You're looking for the Autopista, the Tijuana-Ensenada toll road.

## Stuff For Kids

- Movie studio, beaches, surfing and general Mexico fun makes it a great — but long — day for older kids.

## Stuff For Adults

- Art galleries, great bars and restaurants, romantic hotels... maybe you should leave the kids at home.

**M**any San Diegans are experienced Mexico drivers; I was escorted by one, my friend, Delena Cozart. A couple of years ago, she and her white Mazda Miata, named "Simón Blanco," ventured all the way to Puerto Vallarta. It's about a four-day drive including a 10-hour ferry trip from Baja to the mainland, but that's another story.

Delena picked an easy route, mostly on the toll road, but with a detour south of Rosarito Beach past the Fox Baja Studio, through an artists' colony and by many historic sites.

She advises caution on Avenida Internacíonnal in Tijuana. Cars tend to drive too fast along the first stretch, having to slam on the brakes when encountering a slow-moving truck or bus.

After crossing the border, stay right to follow the "Scenic Road" signs. Stay right except to pass, as it's the law on Autopista. There are also some pesky left-merging onramps that can be a surprise.

### On The Road

- Be sure to get insurance before entering Mexico. U.S. insurance usually doesn't apply in Mexico.

- Traffic laws and driving methods are different in Mexico.

- On the "free road," off the Autopista, pavement can be a bit rough.

- Lots of trucks on the "free road."

- Don't drive at night.

**For more Mexico driving tips, see pages 130-131.**

**O**ver the hills are the ocean, the Playas de Tijuana neighborhood and Bullring by the Sea. On the U.S. side is the Border Field State Park (see Drive 11).

Continue following the signs to Ensenada and the first of three Casetas de Cambio, or toll stops, at about the 10-kilometer mark. The toll varies, but on our visit it was $2.20 U.S. at each location. The friendly toll takers accept pesos and U.S. dollars. Each toll plaza also has clean rest rooms and tourist information. In

**Hotels dot the coast at Rosarito Beach.**

**Hotel Calafia sits atop rugged cliffs.**

case you're worried about safety, there are emergency telephones every couple of kilometers, several rest areas, and police patrols. It's a nice drive.

The geography of the northern Baja coast resembles San Diego's North County area, rising quickly from the ocean to the coastal hills. Development is pretty constant from Tijuana to Rosarito Beach, 18 kilometers south.

The old Rosarito Beach Hotel is accessible through an Autopista exit at the 21 km mark; at one time this was the only tourist facility around. Neimann says the hotel and casino were built in 1926, and were taken over in 1929 by the legendary Manuel Barbachano. It is still run by his nephew, onetime Rosarito mayor Hugo Torres Chabert.

Now a city, Rosarito Beach is one of the worldwide hot spots for college-student vacations, with numerous high-rise hotels now along the coast. We avoided the hubbub, exiting the Autopista just south of Rosarito at the next Caseta de Cambio.

Marked for La Paloma, Popotla, and Calafia, it's the last exit for several kilome-

*Rubbernecker Special*

- First-timers can't believe the views.
- Old-timers can't believe the development.
- Cultural differences can be great, but the distance back home isn't.

Legend:
1. Libramiento Oriente
2. Avenida Baja California
3. Boulevard Lazero Cardenas
4. Carretera Al Aeropuerto
5. Avenida Tijuana Zona Industrial

## Directions

- Interstate 5 or 805 to International Border.
- Follow signs to "Scenic Road," Mexico Highway 1-D, the Autopista Ensenada Tijuana.
- Take La Paloma/Popotla/ Calafia exit.
- Turn left (south) to continue on Mexico Highway 1 (free road). Watch for construction.
- Return to Autopista toll road (Mexico 1-D) southbound at La Fonda.

- Entering Ensenada, keep right to Boulevard Azueta for the harbor area; left to Bahia de la Paz for downtown shopping district.
- Return via Autopista 1-D.

### U.S. Return

#### Otay border crossing

- Exit Autopista at Costa Azul, following signs to La Mesa neighborhood of Tijuana over Carretera Al Porlado La Gloria.

- Right at Libramiento Oriente. Continue onto Avenida Baja California, Boulevard Lazaro Cardenas and Carretera Al Aeropuerto.
- Right at Avenida Tijuana Zona Industrial to Otay Border Crossing.

#### San Ysidro border crossing

- Follow signs at end of Autopista to U.S., via Segunda Benito Juarez through downtown Tijuana.

DRIVE 14

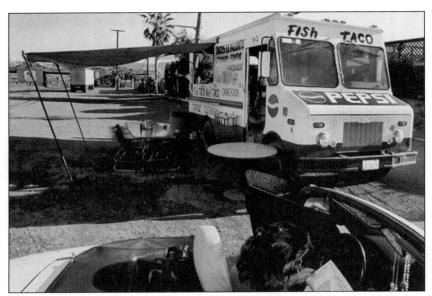

**Setup at 52 km looks temporary but they've been serving tacos for years.**

## *Mexico Tips*

Mexico is a foreign country, so be aware there are different laws, particularly on the highway. Here are some tips for driving south of the border:

- **Insurance:** Most U.S. insurance policies are invalid in Mexico. Agencies selling Mexican insurance are along the U.S. approaches to the border. When getting insurance, make sure the insurance agent or company has a 24-hour service telephone number in Mexico. Why? You may need to contact your insurance agent outside of normal business hours, and may not be able to call the U.S. Also, keep a copy of the phone number and policy number with you at all times; if you store it in the car's glove compartment and the car is stolen, you're in big trouble.

- **Inspections:** Mexico, like the United States, operates an inspection station at border crossings. Most cars are passed through and there's usually not the traffic backup seen heading north. There are

ters and the ramp to take to visit the coastal colonias, artists and furniture shops, and the Fox Baja Studios.

Watch for ongoing construction in this area. When completed, the road will be four lanes… as wide as the Autopista and a great improvement for residents and visitors alike.

First up is the Fox Baja Studio, built for the blockbuster "Titanic" and continuing as a busy movie location. "Foxploration" tours are available daily.

Many local residents have stories about the actors and actresses working there… just ask in any of the local restaurants or businesses.

Next, we bounced off the road to Punta Descanso, home

Except for the tolls, Autopista is just like California's freeways.

of the Hotel Calafia. Hugging the coast at 35.5 km from Tijuana, the restaurants and hotel rooms offer spectacular ocean views. Guests can also get a history lesson, as the complex has been declared a local historic landmark. One of the dining rooms has memorabilia from the "Titanic" movie and even serves a menu from the original voyage.

Art studios, furniture stores and restaurants line this stretch of the free road, including the Georgio Santini Gallery at the 40 km mark. Named for the inventor of the Caesar salad and now operated by his son, the gallery boasts a modern collection. Even if you're not a collector, a stop is recommended just to see the ocean views from the galleries and adjacent colonia.

You don't have to worry about places to eat along the way. We stopped for lunch at a roadside food truck that served great fish tacos.

If you're not so adventuresome, there are numerous restaurants, including about

also checkpoints on interior roads, similar to those on the U.S. side.

- **Night Driving:** Avoid it. Lighting is poor or nonexistent off the toll road; even on the toll road it can be intermittent. Pedestrians, bicycles, and livestock are also hazards at night.

- **Metric System:** Distances along the roadways are marked in kilometers, about five-eighths of a mile. Most speedometers have kilometers-per-hour markings... those are the little numbers next to the big miles-per-hour. Down the peninsula, many landmarks, restaurants, hotels, and other businesses are marked by their distance from the border in kilometers (.62 km per mile.

- **More Information:** If you're doing any driving in Mexico, check out one of the tour books. For example, the American Automobile Association's "Mexico Travel Book" devotes more than 10 pages to driving in Mexico, including information on laws, government tourist services, and things to avoid.

**Fantastic view from El Mirador rest area. Below, keep track of the kilometers.**

three dozen in the community of Puerto Nuevo, famous for its lobster; the Halfway House, which Niemann describes as "the first and only bar" between Tijuana and Ensenada when it opened in 1922; and the restaurant La Fonda, just a bit further south on a bluff top.

We rejoin the Autopista just before the town of La Mision, where the free road heads inland. We'll stay on the coast, past several oceanfront communities, including the Bajamar Resort. Mostly, the volcanic coastal hills gently slope toward the water, with spectacular cliffs falling off abruptly into the surf, but there's also an area of beach-side sand dunes, popular with off-roaders.

Just past Bajamar is the El Mirador Rest Area, the best of many stops along the way. The restaurant and other facilities are closed, but the rest rooms were open when we visited. High on a cliff above the ocean, El Mirador offers one of the most spectacular views on the Autopista; pull off and enjoy.

Entering Ensenada, we stopped for a quick bite to eat at the Hotel Punta Morro, which occupies a skinny strip of land next to the Ensenada campus of the Universidad Automa de Baja California. The sunset view from the rocky

**Sunset from the patio of the Hotel Punta Morro.**

point was fantastic, even by Southern California standards.

In town, we stayed to the right, following the signs to the Centro, or downtown, through the industrial portion of this busy port city. Make a right at the Pemex gas station to Boulevard Costero, the fish markets, and waterfront.

From there, we walked to the Riviera del Pacifico, a 1920s vintage hotel and casino restored and now a local cultural center, the Centro Social, Civico Y Cultural de Ensenada. It's a popular spot for local weddings and other parties. Restoration of the hotel was a longtime civic effort; wall tiles commemorate individuals and companies that helped.

**W**ith **370,000 people**, Ensenada is a bustling city. Its downtown runs east from the port, with shopping along Avenida Lopez Mateos, Boulevard Azueta, and Avenida Ruiz. Looking across the Bahia de Todos Santos, you'll see La Bufadora (The Snorter), which marks the edge of the bay. A few miles to the south, it's a hollow rock formation that snorts water when the tides are right.

Our day over, we headed back north on 1-D and the biggest challenge, crossing the border. At Costa Azul, Baja California 1 (the free road) and 1-D (the toll road) cross, with Baja California 1 heading east to Tijuana's La Mesa neighborhood. We opted to take Baja California 1, cutting through town to the Port of Entry on Otay Mesa. It took us an hour to cross, not bad for a Saturday evening.

Baja California is truly different world. It's close and offers spectacular scenery unique in the world. The food isn't bad, either and it's great to get a dose of another culture, right here in our back yard. Enjoy your drive.

## *For More Information*

- **Fox Baja Studios,** Km 32.5 Carretera Libre Tijuana-Ensenada, Centro Turístico Popotla, Rosarito, B.C., Mexico, (866) 369-2252, *www.foxploration.com*, *www.foxbaja.com.* Movie studio open for tours daily.

- *Gringo Gazette,* an English-language Baja newspaper, has all

**Unique Taco Surf shop sign near Rosarito.**

  sorts of up-to-date information, *www.gringogazette.com.*

- **Bajalife.com,** a commercial web site offering tours, hotel reservations and other information, *www.bajalife.com.*

- **Hotel Calafia,** Km 35.5, Autopista Tijuana-Ensenada, (877) 700-2093, *www.hotel-calafia.com.* Historic cliffside hotel and restaurant complex.

- **Rosarito Beach-Ensenada Web Site,** *www.rosarito-ensenada.com.* Commercial site with events listing, restaurants, hotels and other points of interest in the Baja region from Rosarito Beach to Ensenada.

- **Planet Baja,** *www.planetbaja.com.* Spanish-language site with entries to many other local Baja California web pages.

## Drive 15

# Russians, Wineries, and the Real Baja

### The Valleys from Ensenada to Tecate

**O**n the list of roads less traveled, the route from Ensenada to Tecate has to rank as one of the best.

Most Americans are familiar with Tijuana, just across the border from San Diego. A bustling, cosmopolitan city, it's connected to the seaport at Ensenada by a superhighway. Development stretches most of the 62 miles (100 kilometers) south.

This part of the Baja coast is very international. Spotting license plates from the

### Distance

- About 73 miles from El Sazul to Tecate.

- U.S.-Mexico border (Tijuana) to El Sazul is about 60 miles.

- Another 40 miles from Tecate to San Diego.

DRIVE 15

**Take Highway 3 and stay on it all the way to Tecate.**

U.S. isn't difficult; many Americans call this area home.

The contrast couldn't be greater just a little bit to the east. Tecate, just 35 miles from Tijuana, is still a traditional, mid-sized Mexican city. Its connection to Ensenada is much more typical of travel through this nation — two lanes, twisting, and sometimes lonely.

Today we're exploring this very scenic and unique road, Baja California Highway 3.

Drivers from San Diego have several choices when beginning this trip, since our route only covers the one-way trip between Tecate to Ensenada.

I opted to take the fast way down and the slow, twisting route back. I headed south from Tijuana to Ensenada over the Autopista, the toll road. It takes a little more than an hour from the border and we experienced the spectacular expressway (see Drive 14) at full speed.

*Stuff For Adults*

- Wineries, a brewery, history, and shopping make a great day for the grown-ups.
- Kids would probably get bored.
- Think about having a designated driver.

By going south-to-north, we took advantage of the smaller, normally less congested U.S. port of entry at Tecate. From there, it was a quick drive over California's SR-94 (see Chapter 4) back to San Diego.

The road to Tecate begins in the northern Ensenada industrial neighborhood of El Sauzal, home to a fragrant seafood packing plant. The view improves as the smell subsides.

My guides along the two tours were Bill Swank, a San Diego author and baseball historian, and Bertha Sandoval, the public relations director for the Tecate Brewery, officially the Cerveceria Tecate.

Bill's been knocking around Baja since the 1960s and Bertha's a Tijuana native who has a couple of brothers that own ranches in the area.

Our trip up Baja Highway 3 (plus a few side-trips) is a 73-mile journey through three major valleys and the rolling hills in between. Small towns dot the landscape every few miles. The first up is San Antonio de las Minas, just a few miles north of the turnoff at El Sauzal.

Bertha and I stopped for lunch at Leonardo's restaurant, a popular local eatery that was full on a Saturday morning. As is common for many restaurants catering to the native population, a full lunch cost

## On The Road

- Be sure to get Mexican insurance for your car. See Chapter 14.

- Be vigilant on narrow, two-lane road.

- Wide spots are infrequent, but take advantage of them to enjoy the view.

- One military checkpoint in Guadalupe Valley.

- Don't cut the border line in Tecate.

- Gas up before leaving San Diego, but just in case there are several Pemex stations along the way.

- Watch for speeding semi's and slow moving vehicles.

**Las Minas de San Antonio Restaurant is in a plant nursery.**

**Wonderful turns as highway heads north from San Antonio de las Minas.**

half of what it might at one of San Diego's bargain Mexican restaurants. The desserts are also wonderful.

Off the main highway a bit is the Las Minas de San Antonio Restaurant y Vivero, a plant nursery with a restaurant open for breakfast and lunch. We didn't try the food but it has a great reputation.

Heading north again on the Carretera a Tecate-El Sauzal (Highway 3), the road continues climbing and twisting through the coastal foothills. This stretch is very enjoyable driving, with gentle curves.

We visited in the spring. The hills were green and the flowers were in bloom. Summer can be very hot in these valleys, so the ever present coastal breeze at our back was very welcome. There wasn't very much traffic either on a weekday or Saturday. That's a big change from the busy coastal route.

*Nature Lovers Ride*

- Breathtaking vistas of valleys and rolling hills.
- Fascinating history around every turn.
- Wildflowers and green hills in the Spring; nurseries and vineyards year-round.

About 20 miles north of Ensenada is the town of Valle de Guadalupe, the center of the Guadalupe Valley. In his fascinating book, *Baja Legends*, author Greg Niemann reveals that area has been inhabited by humans for thousands of years. Kumeyaay Indians — ancestors of tribes in San Diego County — called it Oja Cuñurr, or Painted

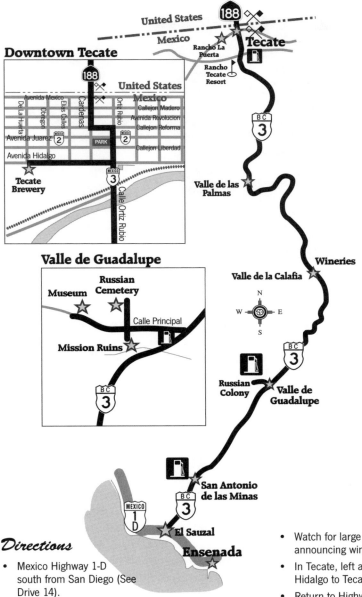

## Directions

- Mexico Highway 1-D south from San Diego (See Drive 14).

- Baja Highway 3 north from El Sauzal.

- In Valle de Guadalupe, left at Pemex station to museum on Calle Principal.

- The cemetery is north from four-way stop; mission ruins are south.

- Return to Highway 3, north.

- Watch for large signs announcing wineries.

- In Tecate, left at Aveneda Hidalgo to Tecate Brewery.

- Return to Highway 3 (Calle Ortiz Rubio) and head north toward border. Follow directional signs to border crossing.

- In U.S., take SR-188 to SR-94 (see Chapter 4).

DRIVE
15

**San Diegan Bill Swank, left, talks with Guadalupe Valley museum curator.**

Caves, based on some now-destroyed cave art in the area.

In 1905, a group of 500 Russian religious dissidents, called Molokans (milk drinkers), purchased 13,000 acres in the valley. They set up a town and began farming in the region. They brought the first grapes to the valley, which is now the Baja California version of Napa Valley.

Today a few of the relatives of the original Molokans live on in Valle de Guadalupe. A nice, government-run museum tells the story of the Molokans, the Kumeyaay, the Spanish mission that operated in the town for only six years, and the people of the valley.

The old Russian cemetery is nearby, as are the mission's ruins. All spots are worth a visit and getting there, as they say, is half the fun. Streets aren't marked, so just make a left (apparently onto Calle Principal) at the Pemex gas station as you enter the town of Valle de Guadalupe.

After several speed bumps and the pavement becomes dirt (more than a mile from the gas station) you'll see two museum signs. The one on the right (west) side of the road is the government-run establishment, the Museo Historico Valle Guadalupe. Across the road is a private museum in several old homes.

Headed back to Highway 3, the only four-way stop has a small sign pointing to the mission ruins, to the right. To the left is the old Russian cemetery. If you get lost, just ask for directions, as the towns folk and local police are very friendly.

The cemetery includes headstones dating from the 1880s, many in disrepair; with Cyrillic writing, they're easy to spot.

At the other end of the road, the mission's ruins are fenced. An information sign, in Spanish, tells of the short life (1834-1840) of the church.

Back on the main highway, wineries and vineyards appear as you enter the Guadalupe Valley and on over the hills toward Valle de las Palmas.

As we head into wine country and toward beer country (Tecate), just a note about taking alcoholic souvenirs back into the United States. There are limits to the amount of beer and wine travelers can bring back into the U.S. without paying customs duty. Anything more than a liter (about a quart) may cost you at the border.

The biggest wineries in the valley, L.A. Cetto and Domecq, are across the road from each other. Domecq has a $3 per car entry fee and includes extensive caves cut into the surrounding hill.

The caves, similar to those at wineries in Northern California and France, provide just the right temperature for aging wine, even in hot Baja summers. As with all the Baja wineries open to the public, wine tasting and sales are available.

L.A. Cetto is about a mile off the highway, via a pleasant, gravel road through the vine-

**Old cemetery has Russian roots.**

L.A. Cetto winery has its own bullring.

yards. Roses are planted at the end of many grape rows; they're there to give advance warning of disease, as the bugs will attack the roses before the grapes.

A modern visitors center features a long bar for tasting. Tours are also available through the large processing facility. Don't miss a drive up the hill to the picnic area and bullring.

Leaving the wineries, the road heads north into the foothills as we near Tecate. The pavement can be washboard-like at times and there are many spots without shoulders, so be careful. The sharpest curves are also in this area.

Views of the rocky hillsides are spectacular, like the area on SR-94 east of Campo, but on a larger scale.

We've now driven more than 60 miles since the turnoff near Ensenada and

Kilometer signs mark distance from Tecate.

**Road winds through rocky countryside between valleys.**

there are many more residences plus signs of one of Tecate's major industries. It's the "mile of tile," a series of tile factories that have drawn designers from all over the world — even home improvement guru Bob Villa.

If you've got room in the car, and enough energy left, load up on some of the fine craftsmanship. And here's a tip from Bertha... the further the shop is located from Tecate, the lower the prices.

Entering town, continue north on Highway 3 until you pass the river. Turn left at Aveneda Hidalgo for a visit to the signature industry in this border town, the Tecate Brewery. Beer tasting and tours are available daily except Sunday.

The large, modern facility is the third largest brewery in Mexico and is owned by FEMSA, Mexico's beverage conglomerate. Brands produced at the Cerveceria Tecate are Tecate, Carta Blanca, Superior, Dos Equis, Bohemia, and Sol.

This is big-time brewing, on the scale of Anheuser Busch and Miller. The half-hour tour includes a video on the company and a walk through the huge cooking tanks and other facilities.

**Tecate Brewery dominates local skyline.**

**Town square in Tecate is ringed by restaurants.**

From the brewery, downtown Tecate is within walking distance, with Parque Hidalgo, shops, and restaurants. The U.S. border crossing is nearby.

Over the 70-plus miles, we've experienced a real slice of Mexico, with rich history, great scenery, fantastic driving, and bustling industry. For any visitor, it's a real treat.

## *For More Information*

•**Mexico Driving Tips**: See Chapter 14.

**Wineries and the Brewery**

- **Wineries Overview**, at the Baja Web site, *www.baja-web.com*
- **L.A. Cetto Winery**, Km 73½ Carretera Tecate-El Sauzal, Valle de Guadalupe, (646) 15-52264, *www.lacetto.com*. Modern winery and vineyards with tasting room and tours. Tasting room and cellars are also located in Tijuana.
- **Domecq Winery**, Km 73, Carretera Tecate-El Sauzal, Valle de Guadalupe, *www.domecq.com.mx*. Large winery and tasting room includes cellars open to the public. Tasting room also located in Ensenada.
- **Tecate Brewery**, beer garden and tours, Avenida Hidalgo and Calle Elias, Tecate, 011-52-665-654-9478 and 011-52-665-654-9490, *www.ccm.com.mx*. Beer garden open noon to 5 p.m., Monday-Friday, noon to 2 p.m. Saturday. Tours are daily except Sunday at noon and 3 p.m., other times with reservations.

## Section 4

# The East and North

### Exploring the Anza-Borrego Desert, Southern Riverside and Orange Counties

**Where else than** this southwestern corner of America can explorers drive from the desert's sands, through farms and agriculture, and end up at the beach all in a few hours?

This group of drives can lets you do just that. Begin in the spectacular Anza-Borrego Desert, then cruise through extreme northern San Diego County and southern Riverside County. Hop over rugged mountains into Orange County, and experience the genesis of the mainland's surf culture.

These routes probably shouldn't — or can't — be done all in the same day, but they'll give you a look at the great variety that is Southern California.

First off is our Desert Daze, a trip around the Anza-Borrego Desert State Park. It's an area so unique that parts are indescribable.

The arid expanse in northeastern San Diego County is home to an unforgiving desert, complete with rugged rock formations, shifting sands, incredible heat, and spectacular vistas.

Then it's off to a loop around Rice Canyon, Temecula, and De Luz, some of the most rugged mountains in Southern California. Although country estates are encroaching into the hills and subdivisions have taken over the valleys, the route we'll follow is still mostly agricultural.

Our tour of contrasts continues with a cruise down the surf highway, California's Highway 1, from Seal Beach to San Clemente. Fans of the Beach Boys will recognize many of the towns along the way from the song "Surfin' Safari" and other tunes from the surf culture of the early 1960s.

Southern Riverside County is full of surprises, with vintage streetcars, more farms and food, a cheese factory, and wineries to explore. The route through Perris and Winchester into Temecula is a surprise even to many residents of the area.

Finally, we cruise over Ortega Highway, the twisting SR-74 through the San Juan Creek gorge, a continuation of the coastal range mountains we explored on the De Luz and Palomar drives.

Around every curve, there's something new to explore. Have a wonderful time.

## *Drive 16*

# Desert Daze

### *Tracing History Through Anza-Borrego*

**O**ne of the great things about living in San Diego is that in about an hour, you can drive from the coast to the mountains to the desert, which is where we're headed today.

Borrego Springs is the northeastern outpost of San Diego County, an oasis at the edge of the Colorado Desert, which extends east to Arizona.

The desert offers its own unique ecosystem, and its roads offer challenging driving. If you haven't been there — what have you been doing with yourself?

Today's drive is one of the longest —

### *Distance*

- About 161 miles from I-15 to I-8.
- Allow an hour from central San Diego via I-15 to the Pala Road exit.
- Another 1.25 hours back to San Diego from Ocotillo Wells and I-8 interchange.

DRIVE
16

**Montezuma Valley Road cuts through rugged hills.**

about 161 miles, plus the distance from your home up Interstate 15 to Pala Road and back home from Ocotillo over Interstate 8 (my round trip from downtown San Diego was 250 miles). Budget the whole day, or make it a weekend… there are plenty of hotels and campgrounds to overnight in Borrego.

There are several ways to get to Borrego Springs, but I prefer the Montezuma Grade, County Highway S-22. From I-15, take Pala Road (SR-76) east past Lake Henshaw. Then make a left at SR-79, and a right at San Felipe Road (S-2). A left at Montezuma Valley Road will take you down to Borrego Springs.

Other ways to Borrego Springs are to continue down San Felipe Road, or to take SR-78 through Julian. I prefer Montezuma Valley Road because it generally has less traffic and goes right into Borrego Springs.

**O**pened in 1964 to provide a direct link to Borrego Springs, Montezuma Valley Road twists down the hill from the small farming community of Ranchita. According to Diana Lindsay's excellent *Anza-Borrego A to Z*, the road took 160,000 tons of dyna-

**Desert overlook from Montezuma Valley Road.**

**View of Borrego Badlands from Fonts Point.**

mite and nearly 10 years to build. The County of San Diego set up a prison honor camp in Ranchita to provide labor, with prisoners hacking out the one million cubic yards of mostly granite to create the grade.

Drivers benefit from its banked curves and turnouts. There are a couple of view points that allow you to observe and learn about the endangered bighorn sheep that live on the rocky cliffs. Beyond lies the desert floor, stretching out endlessly to the east.

The road, like Borrego Springs itself, was the brainchild of A. A. Burnand, who in the years following World War II envisioned another Palm Springs on the site. He brought in investors, including the late James S. Copley, president of the Copley Press, publisher of the *San Diego Union-Tribune*.

Montezuma Valley Road was, according to Lindsay, a compromise that eventually kept Borrego Springs from becoming another Palm Springs. Conservationists feared a major highway would be put through Coyote Canyon to the north and connect with Los Angeles.

Today, Coyote Canyon remains unspoiled. The town and surrounding Anza-

*For The Kids*

- Interactive exhibits at Anza-Borrego Desert State Park Visitor Center.

- Chance to spot bighorn sheep from Montezuma Valley Road.

- Wild West artifacts throughout, especially at Vallecito Stage Stop.

DRIVE 16

## Camping

**State**: The two major campgrounds in the Anza-Borrego Desert State Park are at Borrego Palm Canyon and Tamarisk Grove, plus a primitive camp area at Bow Willow. Horse Camp is at the mouth of Coyote Canyon. For backcountry camping rules, ask park staff. Call (800) 444-7275 for reservations.

**County**: Campsites are available at both the Vallecito and Agua Caliente County Parks.
   Vallecito has 44 primitive campsites, plus additional sites in the youth area.
   At Agua Caliente, there are 140 campsites, many with full or partial hookups. An RV disposal station is also on site.

Borrego Desert State Park stayed isolated and today is a wonderful place to spend a day, week or weekend during the fall, winter or spring months.

This is, after all, a desert. It does get hot in the summer.

**F**or those of you that haven't been, Anza-Borrego is not a place of sand dunes and camels (although camel fossils have been found). It is rocky gorges and plains, remnants of a long-gone lake. If you want dunes, head toward the Arizona border.

The peaks and valleys make for a fascinating landscape. At the base of Montezuma Valley Road is a great place to start, the Anza-Borrego Desert State Park Visitor Center.

Exhibits tell the story of the valley's geography and geology, native plants, and animals. Park rangers can point out places to walk, hike, camp, and off-road with an SUV or other vehicle.

Brochures and other information are

**Sandy river bottom road leads to Fonts Point.**

**The lonely road near the Vallecito Stage Station.**

available at no charge.

If you're lucky enough to hit the desert in the spring (following a wet winter), it is transformed from its usual grey/brown/white to amazing colors as the wildflowers bloom. For those who say we don't have the changing of the seasons in Southern California... well, they don't have desert flowers.

**E**ven if you know where you want to go, the Visitor Center is the place to start, as it has an invaluable status board showing the trails that are open for driving, hiking, and horseback riding – and their condition.

For example, I actually drove the dirt road to Fonts Point, which we'll visit later, in a Mazda Miata. But that was in the spring, when rain had packed the sandy soil.

Early in the winter, when it had been dry for months, the same road was a challenge in a four-wheel drive Jeep Wrangler equipped with fat tires.

Another good spot to visit is the Anza-Borrego Desert Natural History Association. It's located on Palm Canyon Drive just before you hit Christmas Circle, the

## On The Road

- Mostly an easy drive on paved roads (with a few twists).

- Optional sandy off-road segments need four-wheel drive.

*A Must For Locals*

- Exploring San Diego's dry eastern edge is a rite of passage for anyone wanting to be a "local." Whether it's off-roading on the dunes, rafting in the Colorado River or touring Anza-Borrego, you aren't a real San Diegan unless you've experienced desert — and beach — sand.

roundabout in the center of town.

In addition to an enthusiastic and knowledgeable staff, you can pick up a couple of driving-tour brochures that will help navigate the valley. I took part of one tour, the "Erosion Road," then doubled back to follow another tour, the "Southern Emigrant Trail," down to present-day Interstate 8 and back to San Diego.

I drove Erosion Road as far as Fonts Point, which is past the Borrego Springs Airport, about 11 miles east of town on S-22. A small sign points to the point, which is about five miles south of the Borrego-Salton Seaway portion of S-22.

The sandy road runs through a wash to the point, which provides a spectacular view of the erosion-sculpted Borrego Badlands. The point is today about 200 feet above a fingerlike wash, created by water and wind.

The drive is fun if you're a novice off-roader, providing just enough slippery sand to make you appreciate power to all four wheels. Stay on the road and don't go crazy, just enjoy the drive.

In fact, all the trails are well marked in Anza-Borrego. Plants and animals are protected and, because water is so scarce, the land is easily scarred. My advice: Respect the park, respect nature, and re-

**Old Vallecito Stage Station.**

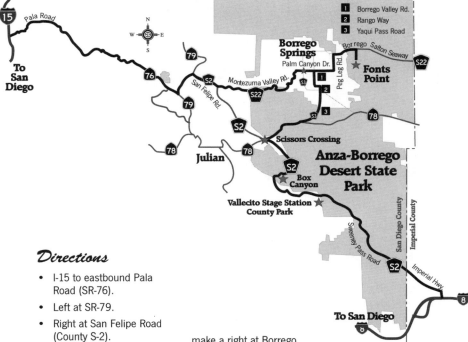

## *Directions*

- I-15 to eastbound Pala Road (SR-76).
- Left at SR-79.
- Right at San Felipe Road (County S-2).
- Left at Montezuma Valley Road (S-22).
- Left at Palm Canyon Road to Anza-Borrego Desert State Park Visitor Center. Check for conditions on dirt roads. If four-wheel drive is recommended and you don't have a four-wheel drive vehicle, I don't advise taking the Fonts Point or Palm Spring side-trips.
- Continue on Palm Canyon Road. Follow S-22 through Christmas Circle in Borrego Springs, around curves on to Pegleg Road and Borrego-Salton Seaway to Fonts Point. If you don't have four-wheel drive,

make a right at Borrego Valley Road and proceed to Scissors Crossing.

- Follow sandy/dirt road to Fonts Point (4 miles). Four-wheel drive may be needed. Check at Anza-Borrego Desert State Park Visitor Center.
- Take S-22 back to Borrego Springs, following road name changes from Borrego Salton Seaway to Pegleg Road to Palm Canyon Drive.
- Left at Borrego Valley Road. Continue on to Rango Way and Yaqui Pass Road, picking up S-3 at Borrego Springs Road. Continue on to Yaqui Pass Road.

- Right at SR-78.
- Left at S-2, (at Scissors Crossing/San Felipe Road).
- Left at Palm Spring (about 26 miles from Scissors Crossing). Sandy road (about 1.5 miles); four-wheel drive may be needed. Check at Anza-Borrego Desert State Park Visitor Center.
- Continue on S-2; changes name at Imperial County line to Imperial Highway.
- Right at Ocotillo Drive.
- West on Interstate 8 to San Diego.

**Looking north on County Highway S-2.**

spect the access that has been granted: stay on the marked roads.

The area is named after Father Pedro Font, a Franciscan Friar who accompanied Spanish Conquistador Juan Bautista de Anza on his explorations through the valley. Anza opened up the desert route that the Spanish used as an overland supply route between Mexico and settlements as far north as San Francisco.

According to Lindsay, from the top of Fonts Point, visitors can see Anza's route as it crossed Borrego Valley and entered Coyote Canyon, en route to the San Gabriel Mission.

"Another more famous route in this desert area is the Southern Emigrant Trail (or County S-2)," said Lindsay, "erroneously signed as the 'Great Southern Overland Stage Route of 1849.' "

The Southern Emigrant Trail became active in 1848 with the discovery of gold in California, but the stage coaches of the Butterfield Overland Mail did not operate until 1858, she said.

Brochures are available at the Natural History Association office and the Visitor Center; or, watch for the signs.

South of Borrego Springs are many spots worth a visit. Box Canyon has spectacular views and a route originally hacked through by the hands of the Mormon Battalion in 1847. Lindsay adds that it was the Battalion who built the first wagon road to California during the Mexican War.

Further on is the restored Vallecito Stage Station. It was one of the stops, reports Lindsay, on the 1858-1861 Butterfield Overland Mail route between Tipton, Missouri, and San Francisco.

Today, the station is the centerpiece of a county park offering picnicking and camping.

Don't miss the left turn to Palm Spring, a bumpy mile off the highway. It's here that Pedro Fages wrote of palm trees in 1782, the first mention of the Southern California symbol by the Spanish.

From there, enjoy the arid hills and valleys down to Ocotillo and Interstate 8. Then it's back over the mountains to San Diego and the ocean.

Southern California... you just can't beat it.

## *For More Information*

- **Anza-Borrego Desert Natural History Association**, 652 Palm Canyon Drive, Borrego Springs, (760) 767-3098, *www.abdnha.org*. Educational facility, bookstore and gift shop run by association volunteers, including knowledgable docents.

### Anza-Borrego Desert State Park Information

- **Visitor Center,** 200 Palm Canyon Drive, Borrego Springs, (760) 767-4205, open daily October through May; weekends, June-September. Wildflower recorded message: (760) 767-4684.

- **Wildflower Post Card Notice,** Park volunteers will let visitors know when to view wildflowers; send a stamped-self addressed postcard to: Anza-

**Off road vehicle is handy in desert.**

DRIVE 16

Borrego Desert State Park, 200 Palm Canyon Drive, Borrego Springs, CA 92004

- **Official State of California Web Site,** Includes link to online campground reservations, Visitor Center, *www.cal-parks.ca.gov* and search for park name.

- **State Park Home Page,** Park activities schedule included: *www.anza borrego.state park.org*

- **Anza-Borrego Foundation**, a nonprofit organization that offers hikes and other events to support preservation of the desert. (760) 767-0446. *www.theabf.org*

**County of San Diego Parks**

- **Agua Caliente County Park,** 39555 County Highway S-2. Geothermally heated springs, spectacular vistas, and miles of trails, plus camping, hiking, and picnicking are available. *www.co.san-diego.ca.us/parks/home.html* and search for park name.

> Font's   Point ➡
> 6.4 km   (4.0 mi)

- **Vallecito Regional Park**, 37349 County Highway S-2. Offers the preserved Vallecito Stage Station, along the Great Overland Stage Route of 1849 (Highway S-2), camping, picnicking, hiking, and other activities. *www.co.san-diego.ca.us/parks/home.html* and search for park name.

**Borrego Springs**

- Chamber of Commerce, *www.borregosprings.org*

**Accommodations**

- Hotels include the Borrego Springs Resort, La Casa Del Zorro resort, and Ram's Hill Resort. Check the Chamber of Commerce site for more accommodations.

**Restaurants/Shopping**

- **Carlee's Place**, 660 Palm Canyon Drive, Borrego Springs, (760) 767-3262. Busy bar/restaurant has hearty food at reasonable prices, entertainment nightly.

- **The Crosswind Restaurant**, Borrego Springs Airport, 1816 Palm Springs Drive, (760)-767-4646. Unusual location for a pretty fair restaurant. Look for the upstairs observation deck.

- Several restaurants and shops are also available in Borrego Springs and at the nearby resorts.

- Outside of Borrego Springs, eating, and shopping is extremely limited. Be sure to pack your own supplies, including plenty of water.

## *Drive 17*

# Doing De Luz

### *Avocados and Twisting Curves in the San Diego-Riverside County Mountains*

**I**n the rugged mountains separating San Diego, Riverside, and Orange counties are testimonials to the determination of both farmers and transportation builders of the 19th and 20th centuries.

Here nature has produced rocky peaks, sheer cliffs, a raging river, and steep gorges.

And yet the work of the agricultural pioneers has resulted in some of the most productive and renowned farmlands in the world, producing avocado and citrus fruit with global demand.

Railroad builders lost out to the temper of the Santa Margarita

### *Distance*

- About 50 miles.
- Allow time to stop for eating and shopping in Old Town Temecula.

DRIVE 17

**Old gas station remains from U.S. 395 days.**

River, robbing National City of its status as the western terminus of the Santa Fe Railroad. It wasn't until the 1970s that a freeway conquered the range.

In between Santa Fe's attempts in the 1880s and the success of Caltrans in the 1970s, a spider web of roads connected Temecula and Escondido.

Many of these roads are still much the same as they were in the early part of the 20th century... just wide enough for two Model Ts to pass. They're narrow, twisting, sometimes banked the wrong way and just right for a great drive.

*Stuff For Adults*

- A romantic drive in the country.
- Shopping in Old Town Temecula and Fallbrook.
- Great, twisty curves for sports cars or motorcycles.
- End the day at the Lawrence Welk Resort.
- Might as well leave the kids at home.

This drive takes a loop through agricultural Rice Canyon, which parallels Interstate 15, via Rainbow. Then it's on to Temecula — no longer just a sleepy farming community — around the rugged Santa Margarita River gorge, and the community of De Luz, through nearly vertical avocado groves. We end up in Fallbrook, another farming community that has grown up.

It's nearly 60 miles of twists and turns, a very challenging route.

From Interstate 15 north of Escondido, take Pala Road east a mile or so to Rice Canyon Road. Horse farms, dairy cattle, and vegetables grow in this narrow valley.

DRIVE
17

Rice Canyon Road today isn't much more than the dirt road connecting farms that it was in the 19th Century.

It twists and turns around the edge of the valley — you don't want a road running through the prime farmland. I drove Rice Canyon Road in my Mazda Miata and sometimes had trouble staying in my own lane... the road is that narrow in spots. So, be careful.

At the top of Rice Canyon Road, make a left at Eighth Street in the community of Rainbow. A quick right puts you on Rainbow Valley Boulevard.

*On The Road*

- Narrow lanes and twisting curves from SR-76 north to Temecula, and from Rancho California Road south to Fallbrook.

- Traffic can be annoying in Temecula and Fallbrook.

- Be careful making left turn onto SR-76 and Sage Road.

According to Lou Stein's *San Diego County Place Names*, Rainbow was founded in 1888 by J.P.N. Rainbow, who took the suggestion of original homesteader, Peter Larsen, and named the settlement after himself.

**Rainbow Valley Road runs through shady grove.**

The story goes that Mr. Rainbow won a seat on the San Diego County Board of Supervisors in 1890. Shortly thereafter, Riverside County was created out of the northeastern part of San Diego County. It ended up that J.P.N.'s house was in the new Riverside County, while his barn was in San Diego county.

J.P.N refused to move into the barn and quit the board.

Today, Rainbow is a small agricultural

**Old Town Temecula has a wild west look.**

community, with several nurseries and stables. Old U.S. 395 — I-15's predecessor — once came through here; a remnant is an old gas station, now shuttered. When you drive by, imagine how you'd squeeze a Ford Excursion up to the pump if it was still a Richfield or Flying A station.

Just into Riverside County, you'll reach an odd, scissor-shaped intersection. If you continue straight, you'll drive through the pleasant little settlement and then loop back onto Rainbow Valley Boulevard. Or, just stay to the right to bypass.

Here's an alert... in rural areas, Riverside County doesn't use street signs. The names of the roads are painted on the sides of white, square poles; sort of adds to the rural flavor.

Next we'll wind through a tree-lined gorge. If you can, pull over in a wide spot in the road, turn off the engine and just listen. If there's water, Rainbow Creek runs just to the left of the road, creating that wonderful babbling brook sound.

The gorge opens up to the Temecula Creek golf course and suburbia... pink stucco houses with red tile roofs. Make a left at Temecula-Pala Road (S-16), then a left at SR-79.

Temecula and Rancho California start here and continue north. We're just passing through, but this could be any suburb anywhere. Continue west on 79, crossing under Interstate 15 and curving right into Front Street and Temecula's Old Town. If you look quick, you'll see the beginnings of the Santa Margarita River, which we'll cross

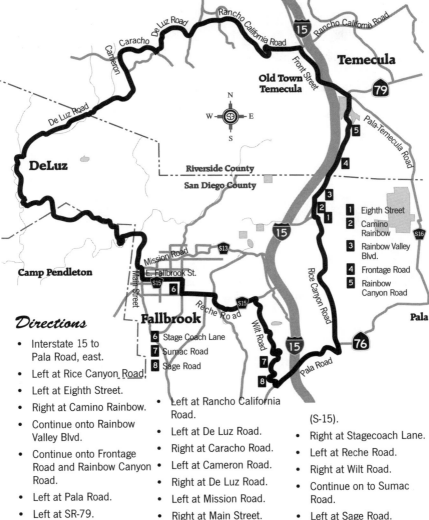

## Directions

- Interstate 15 to Pala Road, east.
- Left at Rice Canyon Road.
- Left at Eighth Street.
- Right at Camino Rainbow.
- Continue onto Rainbow Valley Blvd.
- Continue onto Frontage Road and Rainbow Canyon Road.
- Left at Pala Road.
- Left at SR-79.
- Continue onto Front Street, Temecula.

- Left at Rancho California Road.
- Left at De Luz Road.
- Right at Caracho Road.
- Left at Cameron Road.
- Right at De Luz Road.
- Left at Mission Road.
- Right at Main Street.
- Left at Fallbrook Street

(S-15).
- Right at Stagecoach Lane.
- Left at Reche Road.
- Right at Wilt Road.
- Continue on to Sumac Road.
- Left at Sage Road.
- Left at Pala Road (SR-76)

later.

Old Town Temecula sports restaurants, antique stores, and piped-in music on the streets. There's a wild west theme honoring the town's 1859 founding.

Continue to Rancho California Road and climb up into the mountains. There are several wide spots on the way up that will give you a view of the valley, with its checkerboard of homes, remaining agri-

**De Luz Road fords streams in beautiful gorges.**

cultural areas (including the fine wine country), and mountains to the east.

De Luz Road begins at a "T" intersection with Rancho California Road and is a thrill ride over and around the hilltops. About two miles down the road, a detour (at this writing) sends drivers over Caracho Road and up into the hills.

## Nature Lovers Ride

- Farms, creeks, and other non-urban treats along Rice Canyon Road and Rainbow Valley Road.
- Santa Margarita River gorge is an open space preserve.
- Just forget about urban areas in Temecula and Fallbrook.

Caracho takes a route through the avocado and citrus groves and is a working farm road. It also offers a great vista of the near-vertical groves in the area.

Turn left at Cameron Road, which quickly twists down to its junction with De Luz Road and the other end of the detour. A short way ahead and you're back in San Diego County, where De Luz Road becomes De Luz Murietta Road.

Here you'll alternate between hillsides and creek bottoms, shaded by natural oak groves.

About 11 miles since your turn onto De Luz Road from Cameron, travelers skirt

Camp Pendleton and the edge of the Santa Margarita Ecological Reserve. Here, De Luz Road runs along the edge of the rugged gorge, offering a spectacular view of the last free-flowing river in Southern California, the Santa Margarita.

The Ecological Reserve, which has drawn researchers from all over the world isn't open to the public. At this writing, Tom Chester runs the reserve's docent program, which provides occasional tours of the area. Otherwise, it's closed to the public.

*Side Trip*

- The Lawrence Welk Resort is on your way back to San Diego and worth a visit. Exhibits honor the late band leader, plus there are shops, restaurants, a golf course, and a dinner theater.

**See "For More Information" for location.**

From here, drivers cross a wooden bridge and motor up the hill into Fallbrook. At Sandia Creek Road, you'll pick up the original Santa Fe right-of-way heading into Fallbrook.

Then it's a left and right down Main Street through downtown. Follow S-15 past Live Oak Park to one final thrill ride, the Wilt-Sumac-Sage roads through the hills back to Pala Road and SR-79. It's then just a few minutes to I-15.

This has been one challenging 50 miles, through some of the

**Wildflowers bloom in Santa Margarita open space area.**

most rugged areas of San Diego County. Agriculture, one
of the industries that brought
settlers to this area, is still
king over most of the route.
And thankfully, that means the
roads are still a lot of fun.
Hope you enjoy it.

## *For More Information*

- **Fallbrook Fresh Web Map**,
  *gate.tfb.com/~missnrcd/
  fresh.html* is a map to the
  nurseries, fresh food
  stands, and other agricultural points of interest in
  the Fallbrook area. Al-
  though created in 1999, it's
  a good starting point for exploring this agricultural
  area.

- **Hong's Flower Nursery**,
  1966 Rice Canyon Rd., Rainbow, (760) 728-2399. Stop

Fountain at Lawrence Welk Resort.

  off for some green stuff for the garden.

- **Temecula Creek Inn,** 44501 Rainbow Canyon Road, Temecula, (877)
  517-1823, *www.temeculacreekinn.com*. Resort and golf course just
  across the Riverside County line.

- **Old Town Temecula,** Front Street, Temecula. Original downtown is
  full of shops and restaurants with a wild-west feel.

- **Live Oak Park**, Reche Road, Fallbrook. Community park has picnic
  areas and playgrounds.

- **Tom Chester:** Local naturalist has Web site with information on area:
  *www.tchester.org*

- **Lawrence Welk Resort,** 8860 Lawrence Welk Drive, Escondido, hotel: (760) 749-3000, *www.welkresort.com/sandiego/default.htm*. Golf,
  dining, shopping, theater and museum are a tribute to the late
  "Champagne Music" conductor.

DRIVE
17

## Drive 18

# Surfin' Highway 1
### Endless Drive Down Legendary Sand

**I have to admit I** was a bit of a nerd growing up. A child in the 1960s, I was wholly unimpressed by the surf culture, even though home was San Diego. My sister, nine years older, was into everything Beach Boys, as were most teen girls in the early 60s.

By the time I came along, this stuff was old hat. What a shame.

California Highway 1 from southern Long Beach to San Clemente is really where America's surf craze began. My sister used to laugh about the kids she saw in land-locked Denver, Colorado, driving around with surfboards strapped to the top of their mom's station wagon.

Beginning in 1962, the Beach Boys, who grew up just a bit inland

### Distance

- About 40 miles from Seal Beach to San Clemente.

- Use SR-22 to Seal Beach Boulevard.

**Huntington Beach and pier.**

in Hawthorne, started singing tunes that put these places on the map. The group's song, "Surf City," is still used as the official anthem for Huntington Beach, the second stop on today's trip. Along the way are many other towns mentioned in the group's songs.

Other singers also memorialized the area, including Jan and Dean, who said there were "two girls for every boy" at Huntington Beach.

And while the Annette Funichello/Frankie Avalon beach movies from the same period might have been filmed on a studio back lot or up in Malibu, the spirit lives on in these beach towns.

**B**y and large they're still towns, at least by Orange County standards. The small, beach-side downtowns are generally in pretty good shape and still separated by parks, river valleys, or other terrain.

Like many of the other roads we've covered, this one has its roots as a main highway. It predates U.S. 101, which, before Interstate 5, was the main north-south highway from San Diego to Los Angeles. Many of the towns were originally fishing and

### Stuff For Kids

- Lots of places to stop and run around on the beach.

- Carnival atmosphere at many piers and arcades.

- Eats range from "county fair food" to theme restaurants to fancy dining establishments all along the way.

## On The Road

- Traffic can be heavy, so take your time.
- Sometimes dangerous mix of rubbernecking tourists, locals, and commuters.
- Not much free parking.

farming villages, eventually connected by railroad in the late 19th century.

There's so much to cover here, I can't begin to describe everything on the roughly 40 miles from Seal Beach to San Clemente. I'll try to hit some of the high points, organized by attraction and from north to south, assuming you're heading back to San Diego after a day visiting relatives or the attractions in the Los Angeles/Long Beach area.

By the way, San Diegans will be surprised at the differences facing visitors to beaches and parks to the north. There's almost no free parking and no alcohol is allowed. Maybe that's why Interstate 5 is clogged on the weekends with southbound traffic... residents to the north are taking advantage of our free parking and lax booze rules.

### Beaches

Among the best in the world, most of the beaches here are wide and well developed for visitors; we'll review a few go from north to south along SR-1. Bolsa Chica is more than two miles long, and just north of Huntington Beach.

The two Huntington Beaches — one operated by the city, the other by the state of California — are long, wide and full of fire rings, volleyball courts,

**Strolling on Huntington Beach pier.**

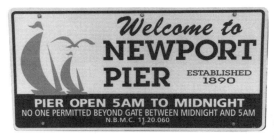

and boardwalks.

The Wedge, considered heaven for bodysurfers is on the southern end of the Balboa Peninsula. It's surrounded by other sand paradises at the north end of the Balboa Peninsula, and south to Corona Del Mar and the Little Corona State Beach.

Further down the coast are the Crystal Cove State Park, Laguna Beach, and Aliso. Salt Creek, Doheney, and two beaches in San Clemente round out the route.

And don't forget change for the parking meters.

**Parks**

Of course, beaches are parks, but even with all the intense development along these 40 miles some natural areas have been preserved.

The largest is the Crystal Cove State Park, stretching beyond the Coast Highway and into the hills. Its 2,000 acres include everything from wooded canyons to a 3.5 mile beach front and an underwater park.

Just south is Heisler Park, home to some of the coast's best tide pools. Located at the bottom of the cliffs below Cliff Drive in Laguna Beach, it includes places to walk, sit and relax and enjoy the

**View of Newport Beach from pier.**

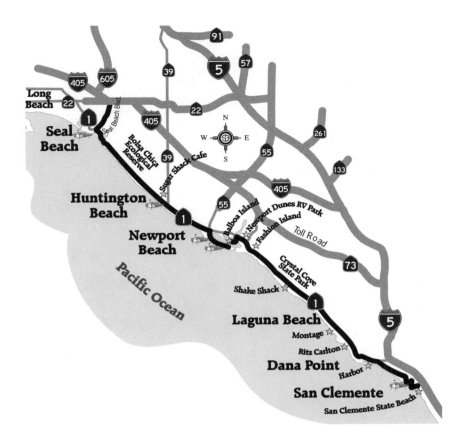

## *Directions*

- Garden Grove Freeway (SR-22) west to Seal Beach Boulevard, south.
- Right at Pacific Coast Highway, SR-1, North.
- Left at Main Street (Seal Beach) to Seal Beach Pier.
- Return to south SR-1.

**Newport Beach/Balboa**

- Right at Balboa Boulevard.

*To Balboa Ferry*

- Right at Palm Street.
- Left at Ocean Front.
- Left at Balboa Boulevard.

- Right at Palm Street to ferry.
- Exit ferry onto Agate Avenue.
- Right at Park Avenue.
- Right at Marine Avenue.
- Right at Pacific Coast Highway, SR-1.

Dana Point/San Clemente

- Take Pacific Coast Highway (right) exit as SR-1 swings east toward Interstate 5.
- Continue onto El Camino Real.

- Right at Avenida Del Mar to San Clemente Municipal Pier, beach and Amtrak station.
- Return to El Camino Real, heading south.
- Right at Avenida Valencia.
- Left at Avenida Del Presidente.
- Right at Avenida Califia to San Clemente State Beach.
- Return to Avenida Del Presidente and Interstate 5.

Fun zone at Balboa.

view. It links with Laguna Beach's downtown Main Beach Park. And don't forget the Laguna Art Museum, right on the coast.

There is a growing network of coastal open space; check the Directory Listings for Web sites from Orange County and the state Coastal Conservancy.

### Piers

From the 1880s to 1920s, when these areas were developed, building a tourist attraction meant sticking a pier into the ocean and putting a dance hall on the end. Roller coasters were also a big attraction.

Railroad tycoon Henry Huntington built the Pacific Electric system, the Los Angeles interurban rail line famous for its red cars. His

*Rubbernecker*
*Special*

- Beautiful vistas, beautiful people all along the route.
- Great way to discover Southern California's surf culture.
- Lots of history.

line stretched south about halfway down our route to Newport Beach (through Huntington Beach, named for the boss) and to attract paying passengers, the areas were promoted as resorts.

**R**emnants of these playgrounds remain today, with piers still braving the Pacific at Seal Beach, Huntington Beach, Newport, and Balboa. The Newport pier location is significant — it was where the McFaddan brothers built a wharf in 1888, before the arrival of the railroad. Soon after, fishermen arrived and started using dories — small, flat-bottomed boats — to ride the Pacific. You'll see references to the dorymen around the pier.

At the nearby Balboa pier, there's a plaque commemorating the first flight to Catalina Island in 1926. It took aviator Glenn Martin 37 minutes to fly the "26 miles across the sea" to the island, breaking all over-water records at the time.

One final pier is at San Clemente, in a unique, cliffside location. The summer-only Amtrak stop is adjacent.

All the piers are worth a visit, with restau-

**Tiny Balboa Island car ferry is a visitors' favorite.**

City Beach at Laguna Beach.

rants, shops and the occasional fun zone. It's still a great escape to stand over the ocean, watching the waves.

### Unique Coastal Attractions

Piers weren't the only things that drew visitors in the 19th and 20th centuries. Dance halls and entertainment midways dotted the coast, and many remain today.

Perhaps the best example is on Balboa Peninsula, where the 1906-vintage Balboa Pavilion still overlooks Newport Harbor. The surrounding Fun Zone has game arcades, shops, and places to eat with everything from salt water taffy to fine dining. There's also a small ferris wheel.

Don't miss the Balboa Island Ferry, which takes cars (three at a time) and pedestrians the one-quarter mile across Balboa Bay to Balboa Island. Just south of Newport Bay, off of Jamboree Road, is the Newport Dunes Waterfront Resort — considered one of the world's most luxurious RV parks.

Laguna Beach is still identified with its roots as an artists colony, sporting many galleries and pottery shops. Don't forget about the annual arts events here, the Pageant of the Masters, the Festival of the Masters, and the Sawdust Festival.

Just south of town are two lavish resorts, the Montage and the Ritz Carlton Laguna Niguel.

### Boating

There is more to enjoying the water along this stretch than just going to the beach. Seal Beach is the inlet to Anaheim Bay and Huntington Harbor. We've already talked about Newport Bay, home to Balboa Island. Down south is Dana Point Harbor.

For boaters, these small anchorages are great places to put down anchor or just get the craft out of the back yard and into the water for the day. There are several boat launches in each that are well marked. Many waterfront restaurants have tie-ups, so you can have a nice cruise and then "tie up" for dinner.

### Shopping and Eating

Starting from Seal Beach, with its funky mix of cafes and shops, through the spruced up Huntington Beach pier area, through Balboa Island and the super swanky Newport Beach, down to artsy Laguna Beach, seafaring Dana Point and funky San Clemente, this route is a shopper's paradise.

Don't miss the exclusive Fashion Island Mall in Newport Beach and shopping for art and pottery in Laguna Beach. Otherwise, take your credit card along and you're on your own.

**T**here are thousands of places to eat along the way, but a few are must-eats. In Huntington Beach, they have a saying that you aren't a real surfer until you've eaten at the Sugar Shack, on Main Street. A diner open for breakfast, lunch, and dinner, they boast that the food is "cooked by surfers, for surfers."

Further down the coast is the Shake Shack, where smoothies and other goodies have been served for 45 years from a ramshackle cliff-top building at the Crystal Cove State Park.

I'm partial to cheeseburgers (as if you haven't figured that out) and ended one of my trips down Highway 1 at Biggie's Burgers in San Clemente.

I've also listed some restaurants recommended by friends in the "For More Information" section at the back of this chapter.

**H**undreds of thousands of cars zip north and south on Interstates 5 and 405 each day. This might be a little slower, and the stoplights can be annoying, but the extra time is well worth it to explore another side of Orange County.

## For More Information

### Cities

- **Seal Beach**, official city site, *www.ci.seal-beach.ca.us.*
- **Huntington Beach,** *www.ci.huntington-beach.ca.us.*
- **Newport Beach**, official city site, *www.city.newport-beach.ca.us.*
- **Laguna Beach**, *www.lagunabeachcity.org*
- **Dana Point,** *www.danapoint.org*
- **San Clemente**, official city site, *www.ci.san-clemente.ca.us.*

### Parks & Beaches

- **California Coastal Conservancy:** Information on coastal habitat, open space and preservation at *www.coastalconservancy.ca.gov.*
- **State Beaches:** Go to State Parks Web site, *www.cal-parks.ca.gov* and search for beach name.
- **Orange County beaches and parks:** See Orange County Parks Web site, *www.ocparks.com.*

### Art Event Information

- **Sawdust Art Festival,** 935 Laguna Canyon Rd., Laguna Beach, (949) 494-3030, *www.sawdustartfestival.org.* Open year-round, artists wares are on display for sale.
- **Festival of the Arts,** 650 Laguna Canyon Road, Laguna Beach, (800) 487-3378, *www.foapom.com.* Summertime events revolving around the Pageant of the Masters.

Dana Point Harbor is a favorite of the yachting set.

**Amtrak runs all year, but only stops at the San Clemente Pier in summer.**

### Restaurants

- **Biggie's Burgers**, 1017 S. El Camino Real, San Clemente, (949) 492-2495. Great cheeseburgers, fries, shakes.

- **Cafe La Fayette**, 330 Main St., Seal Beach, (562) 598-9566. Hearty menu for breakfast, lunch, and dinner. Open daily, except no dinner on Sundays.

- **Cafe Zinc and Market**, 344 Ocean Avenue  Laguna Beach, (949) 494-2791. Simple, health-conscious food is the hallmark of this longtime hangout.

- **Cottage Restaurant**, 308 North Coast Highway, Laguna Beach, (949) 494-3023, *www.thecottagerestaurant.com*. Home-style food in a 1917 vintage home has made this a favorite with locals for years.

- **Coyote Grill,** 31621 South Coast Highway Laguna Beach, (949) 499-6344. Mexican specialties.

- **Crab Cooker,** 2200 Newport Blvd., Newport Beach, (949) 673-0100, *www.crabcooker.com*. Seafood restaurant and market, established 1951, near Newport Pier.

- **Crystal Cove Shake Shack,** 7408 East Coast Highway  Newport Cove, (949) 497-9666. Stop by for a smoothie at a historic surfer hangout.

- **Proud Mary's,** 34689 Golden Lantern, Dana Point, (949) 493-5853. Mary Merrill and family have been dishing up breakfast and lunch to hungry harbor visitors since 1977.

**Body surfers and beachgoers at San Clemente Pier.**

- **Sugar Shack Cafe**, 213 Main Street, Huntington Beach, (714) 536-0355, *www.hbnews.us/shack.html*. Classic beachfront eatery where the customers and employees are all supposed to be surfers.

- **Sundried Tomato and Catering**, 361 Forest Avenue  Laguna Beach, (949) 494-3312, *www.thesundriedtomatocafe.com*. Open for lunch and dinner; a sister location is in Orange.

- **21 Oceanfront,** 2100 West Ocean Front, Newport Beach, (949) 673-2100, *www.21oceanfront.com*. Seafood and other specialties at this fine dining establishment adjacent to the Newport Pier.

**Hotels, Etc.**

- **Hilton Huntington Beach Resort,** 21100 Pacific Coast Highway, Huntington Beach, (714) 845-8000, *www.hilton.com*.

- **Hyatt Regency Huntington Beach Resort and Spa,** 21500 Pacific Coast Highway, Huntington Beach, (714) 698-1234, *www.huntingtonbeach.hyatt.com*.

- **Montage**, 30801 South Coast Highway, Laguna Beach, (866) 271-6953, *www.montagelagunabeach.com*.

- **Newport Dunes Waterfront Resort,** 1131 Back Bay Drive, Newport Beach, (949) 729-3863, *www.newportdunes.com*.

- **Ritz Carlton Laguna Nigel,** One Ritz-Carlton Drive, Dana Point, (949) 240-2000, *www.ritzcarlton.com*.

*Drive 19*

# Wine, Cheese, and Streetcars

## Exploring the Back Roads of Southern Riverside County

**T**he southern part of Riverside County is probably more connected to San Diego today than anytime since the area split off from San Diego County in 1893. Yes, Riverside was once part of San Diego County.

History records that in 1875, a San Diego County Sheriff's posse evicted Native Americans from Little Temecula Rancho lands, moving them east to the hills south of the Temecula

*Distance*

- About 48 miles from Perris to Temecula.

- Perris is about 75 miles north from central San Diego.

River. Descendants of that tribe now run the Pechanga Casino and are among the most influential Native Americans in California.

Today, thousands of commuters make the trek to San Diego jobs from this community where bedrooms are growing like weeds. Most of us living in San Diego just grumble "why would anybody drive that far..." but the Temecula-dwellers say, "we love it."

Well, today we're going to cruise to several of the reasons people like southern Riverside County, with a drive through the rolling hills, a stop at the Orange Empire Railway Museum in Perris, the old town of Winchester, a cheese factory, the new Diamond Valley Lake, Lake Skinner, and the Temecula wine country.

Start off by heading north on Interstate 15, staying right to Interstate 215 in Temecula. Most will recognize I-215 as old U.S. 395, which up to about 10 years ago was the way to

### *For The Kids*

- Trolley rides at the Orange Empire Railway Museum.

- Dairy farms, vegetable stands throughout the drive.

- Cheese making and tasting at Winchester Cheese Company.

- Nature exhibits, fishing, picnicking, camping, and hiking at Lake Skinner.

### *Not For Kids*

- Wineries in Temecula. Tasting and atmosphere are for adults only.

**An old San Diego Electric Railway trolley rests on a siding while a restored Los Angeles Railway car circles the Orange Empire Railway Museum.**

Las Vegas. Signs today direct drivers to stay on I-15 to Vegas, so don't be fooled. It takes a little over an hour to reach the interchange from central San Diego.

**Welcome to the museum.**

A few more minutes up the freeway is the town of Perris. Built by the Santa Fe Railroad back in the 1880s, the boom of southern Riverside County really hasn't yet reached here. But the cheap land and a lot of foresight in the late 1950s made for what is today a real treasure.

**O**ff on the edge of town is the Orange Empire Railway Museum, known to many Southern California rail fans as "the Perris trolley museum." Celebrating rail transit in Southern California, restored and other surviving rolling stock is on display from Los Angeles, the Pacific Electric system and, yes, the San Diego Electric Railway, and the San Diego and Arizona Railroad.

*On The Road*

- Washington Street is a good, twisting country road.

- Highways between Perris and Winchester Cheese Company may have a fair amount of traffic. Pavement condition poor at times.

- If you plan to sample wine, be sure to have a designated driver.

- No designated driver needed after sampling cheese.

Restored streetcars from Los Angeles Transit are open for rides on weekends. Shops and other exhibits are also open, including the Grizzly Flats Railroad, which at one time was in the back yard of the late Disney animator Ward Kimball.

Take a good look at the tracks running along A Street… this was once the Santa Fe Railroad's main transcontinental line, stretching from National City to Chicago. A storm in 1892 wiped out the tracks along the Santa Margarita River (near today's De Luz) and the railroad went to Los Angeles. The rest, they say, is history.

After a time at the museum, head south toward Romoland and Homeland, past I-215. If you see small planes, parachutists, and ultralights, don't worry. It's just the Perris Airport, a hotspot for air sports.

The drive through the hamlets of Romoland and Homeland is not exactly the scenic route, with boxy industrial buildings and homesteads that answer the question, "Just how much junk can you put on an acre?"

After a right turn at SR-79 south (Winchester Road), the scenery and driving conditions improve. Winchester is still very rural, with a convenience store, a good burger spot (Chris Burger), and a few shops. It looks more like a dusty town in the Midwest than something in Southern California.

South of town, look east to the earthen dam of the Diamond Valley Lake. Now nearly full, it is the largest body of water in Southern California, storing drinking water for the Metropolitan Water District, which supplies water to San Diego. It has been called the largest earth-works project ever in the United States.

**J**ust across the highway, stop in at the Winchester Cheese Company for homemade cheese. No, this isn't Wisconsin, but the home of Jules Wesselink, a Dutch native who's been in the dairy business in Southern California since the 1950s.

Natural gouda is the specialty. Visitors can watch cheese being made, usually Tuesdays, Wednesday, and Thursdays from 10 a.m. to 1 p.m., but if you want to make sure the factory's running, they

**Entry to Winchester Cheese Company.**

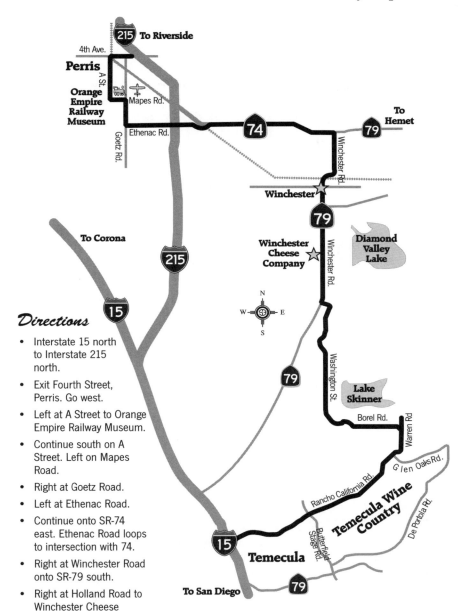

## Directions

- Interstate 15 north to Interstate 215 north.
- Exit Fourth Street, Perris. Go west.
- Left at A Street to Orange Empire Railway Museum.
- Continue south on A Street. Left on Mapes Road.
- Right at Goetz Road.
- Left at Ethenac Road.
- Continue onto SR-74 east. Ethenac Road loops to intersection with 74.
- Right at Winchester Road onto SR-79 south.
- Right at Holland Road to Winchester Cheese Company.
- Return to SR-79 south.
- Left at Washington Street. Continue onto Borel Road.

- Left at Benton Road to Lake Skinner.
- Return to Borel Road and continue south.

- Continue onto Warren Road.
- Right onto Rancho California Road. Continue to Interstate 15 south.

## Rubbernecker Special

- Even some Temecula locals haven't explored this part of their own "back yard."

- Rolling hills surrounded by mountains make for spectacular scenery.

- Includes "only heres" such as the wine country, Southern California's largest lake (Diamond Valley Lake), the cheese factory, and trolley museum.

- Home construction will wipe out much open space in coming years.

advise you to call first. The excellent cheeses are made by Jules's daughter, Valarie, and son-in-law, David.

From a small batch mixed up in a cooler in 1995, the business has grown to 95,000 pounds of cheese a year. Varieties are sold in San Diego at farmer's markets and the Henry's Marketplace chain, plus several hotels and restaurants. Mail order is also available through the Web site.

The rolling hills in this area are especially beautiful in the spring following a wet winter. With mountains visible in all directions, this is a gorgeous valley that from this vantage point still looks unspoiled.

While SR-79 can be busy (it's a main connector between the freeway and Hemet), Washington Street is a fun yet easy drive as it curves around, up, and over terrain. Traffic on a recent Saturday was light, as folks seem to take Rancho California Road from the southwest to reach the wineries and our next stop, Lake Skinner.

Covering more than 6,000 acres, the lake's recreation facilities in-

**Rolling hills from Washington Street.**

**Front gate to Lake Skinner is across from grape fields.**

clude picnic areas, fishing, and camping. Since it's a water source, swimming isn't allowed, but the lake is well worth a visit and the $2 entry fee.

Back on the highway, it's time for wine. Between here and Butterfield Stage Road are 16 wineries, most located on Rancho California Road. All have tasting rooms, some have restaurants. On the weekends, tour buses and rented limos transport tasters between the wineries, and the place has the ambiance of the Gaslamp Quarter on a Saturday night. With a paid designated driver, drinkers can enjoy every sip.

One of the oldest wineries is near the southwestern edge, Callaway, which was founded by Ely Callaway in the 1970s. In those days, there were no housing tracts between the winery and the small Rancho California development near the freeway.

The hills tend to hide all the development to the west, providing fantastic

**Lake Skinner offers fishing, picnicking, camping.**

vistas from the picture windows and patios of the tasting rooms. The coastal breeze — one of the things that makes these great grape-growing grounds — is something to savor along with the wine.

Several wineries are on DePortola Road, which is just southwest of Rancho California Road. Take either Anza Road or Butterfield Stage Road south to DePortola.

Suddenly, you're back in suburbia... beautiful Temecula. The city limits are just west of the Hart Winery and shortly the road widens. Another day in the country has come to an end.

At the rate that suburbs are gobbling up southern Riverside County, much of this open space might be chewed up in a matter of years. Enjoy the wine and cheese while you can.

## *For More Information*

**Orange Empire Railway Museum,** 2201 South A Street, Perris. Telephone: (909) 657-2605 (recorded information) or (909) 943-3020 (live). *www.oerm.org*. Spend a few hours or the day riding vintage trolleys and exploring the grounds.

**Chris Burgers,** 28325 Winchester Road, Winchester. Telephone: (909) 926-2323. Extensive menu of grilled fast food specialties with a family atmosphere.

**Winchester Cheese Company,** 32605 Holland Road, Winchester. Telephone: (909) 926-4239. *www.winchesetercheese.com* Tasting and cheese making in the middle of a working dairy.

**Lake Skinner,** 37701 Warren Road, Temecula. Telephone: General information, (909) 926-1541; campground and reservations, (800) 234-7275; boat rental and concessions, (909) 926-1505; ranger station, (909) 926-3046. *www.ci.temecula.ca.us/homepage/Visitors/skinner.htm* Full service park includes hiking, camping, and fishing.

**Temecula Wineries,** Web site, *www.temeculawines.org* Gateway site includes links to many of the Temecula wineries, directions, and phone numbers for all.

## Drive 20

# Ridin' on the 74

### Ortega Highway — the Scary, Scenic Route from Lake Elsinore to San Juan Capistrano

**F**or many residents of **Orange** and Riverside counties, the Ortega Highway is something to be avoided.

In recent years, the meandering 28 miles from Lake Elsinore to San Juan Capistrano has become an overcrowded commuter route between the bedroom communities of southern Riverside County and the jobs closer to the coast.

Traffic accidents are common. In 2001, the *Los Angeles Times* reported there were nearly 2,000 accidents on the highway from 1995-99. There were 107 people killed

### Distance

- About 40 miles from Lake Elsinore to San Juan Capistrano.

- Drive, with stops, takes about two hours.

- Allow an additional 1.25 hours each direction from central San Diego.

**Lake Elsinore's Diamond ball park.**

and 3,211 seriously injured on the full 44-mile stretch from Perris to San Juan Capistrano.

Problem areas are where the Ortega ascends from Lake Elsinore at Grand Avenue, the Lookout Roadhouse restaurant at the top of the grade, "Ricochet Alley," just west of the Orange County line around Ronald W. Caspers Wilderness Park, and in urban San Juan Capistrano, where the highway meets Interstate 5.

Still, it's worth a visit, as it goes through some of the most rugged and scenic parts of coastal Southern California. It also has a lot of history.

### Stuff For Kids

- Hiking trails, picnic grounds and other opportunities to enjoy nature are all along the Ortega Highway.

- Some kids also enjoy wild curves and watching Mom or Dad white-knuckle the steering wheel.

I opted to go from east to west, starting at Diamond Drive in Lake Elsinore. Exiting Interstate 15, Diamond Drive ends at the fine minor league ballpark, The Diamond. Home of the Lake Elsinore Storm of the California League, this park packs in ball fans from all over the region. It's an enjoyable way to spend a hot summer evening.

Nearby is a great spot for hot dogs, Wild Weenies, 31715 Mission Trail. It's a tiny old-fashioned hot dog stand, one of those spots left over from the days when Elsinore was not much more than a wide spot in the road.

Head north on Lakeshore Drive, then following the main road as it turns right onto Main Street, then make the left at Graham Avenue.

### On The Road

- One of the top ten roads in California for fatalities.
- Drive defensively and conservatively.
- Traffic, traffic, traffic.

At 201 West Graham is the original Crescent Bath House and Hotel, built in 1887 by one of the town's co-founders, Franklin Heald. The spa closed in the 1940s; its most recent use has been as an antique store. The building is also rumored to be haunted.

Graham then merges back with Lakeshore, which will take you to Highway 74, Riverside Drive.

**I**ncorporated in 1888, Lake Elsinore today has about 35,000 residents. The town has been through many ups and downs; it's now part of the bedroom community boom in southern Riverside County. That has lead to the traffic problems on the Ortega.

Before heading up the hill, check out the Lake Elsinore Recreation Area, a park, boat launch and campground at 32040 Riverside Drive. Then, after the turn from Riverside onto Grand Avenue, follow the SR-74 signs onto the Ortega Highway.

The highway quickly climbs about 1,000 feet to the summit at El Cariso. The steep grade offers spectacular views and the first of many blind, hairpin curves.

**Swimming and boating at Lake Elsinore.**

**Lake Elsinore view from the Lookout Roadhouse.**

There are several spots to stop and take in the view. One of the most popular is the Lookout Roadhouse, a restaurant at 32107 Ortega Highway. Open weekdays for breakfast and lunch and all day on weekends, the Lookout serves great ribs along with a fabulous view of the lake below.

The Lookout is popular with the biker set but don't be intimidated by a parking lot full of Harleys; everybody's very friendly.

**L**ake Elsinore disappears from the rearview mirror as the Ortega enters the Cleveland National Forest. Ortega's high point is only 2,666 feet, so the forest is a bit thin. Still, the temperature can be 10-20 degrees cooler than in the valley below.

On the days I drove the highway, the usual "May gray" coastal fog stopped at the summit. From Lake Elsinore, it looked like cotton on top of the mountain.

In the settlement of El Cariso (population around 250) is a Cleveland National Forest visitor information center, a great place to stop and get your bearings.

**Water tank marks summit restaurant.**

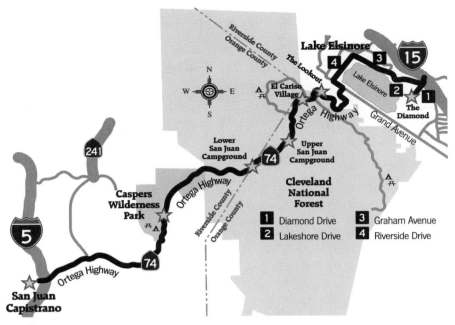

Cleveland National Forest
1 Diamond Drive    3 Graham Avenue
2 Lakeshore Drive   4 Riverside Drive

### Directions

- Interstate 15 to Diamond Drive exit.
- West to Lake Elsinore Diamond.
- Return to Lakeshore Drive. Turn right (north).

- Right at Main Street.
- Left at Graham Avenue. Continue onto Lakeshore Drive.

- Left at Riverside Drive.
- Left at Grand Avenue.
- Right at Ortega Highway (SR-74).

Ortega Highway runs nearly through the middle of the forest's Trabuco District, this northernmost chunk of the federal lands that stretch south nearly to the Mexican border.

**S**everal campgrounds are nestled in the trees: Blue Jay and Trabuco, near El Cariso, Ortega, and Upper and Lower San Juan. Picnic spots are in the Memorial Picnic Area (near El Cariso), Blue Jay, El Cariso North and upper San Juan.

From El Cariso, Killen Trail winds south through the forest to DeLuz, via the Wildomar off-highway vehicle park, campground, picnic areas and hiking trails.

One of the favorite trails in the area is the San Juan Loop Trail, a 2.1-mile walk through oak groves, wildflowers and a waterfall along the San Juan Creek. There are views to the Santa Monica Moun-

**Patty's Place is a popular spot in El Cariso Village.**

tains.

Be sure to use a Forest Service Adventurepass or pay the daily fee to park.

Just a bit down the road is Patty's Place, a small market and gift shop selling its own brand of pork, beef, and other kinds of jerky. There are patio tables out back.

Highway 74 then begins its slow decent to the coast. Following San Juan Creek most of the way, this highway was built in the 1920s and hasn't been upgraded much since. There aren't any tunnels, but any driving enthusiast will be kept busy avoiding the sheer cuts through solid rock, bridges, and the frequent twists and curves.

There are also an estimated 7,000 cars a day using this road, so pay attention.

Watch for cars exiting the campgrounds and other facilities along the way, for cars heading the other direction that may have drifted over the center line and for cars in your own lane whose drivers aren't handling the twists and curves as well as you are.

Oh, and don't forget to keep your car from going over a cliff. Remember, the *Los Angeles Times* called this stretch "Ricochet

*Nature Lovers Byway*

- Despite the traffic, the Cleveland National Forest, San Juan Creek, and Caspers Park are fabulous preserves.

**On the Ortega Highway.**

Alley."

Ronald W. Caspers Wilderness Park is in the beautiful valley and offers 8,000 acres of picnicking, hiking, horseback riding, camping, and mountain bike trails. River terraces and sandstone canyons are filled with native Coastal Live Oak and California Sycamore.

In the spring, streams run and wildflowers bloom. Like the Cleveland National Forest, it's an amazing wild place that is quite a contrast to Orange County's human congestion.

Heading into Rancho Mission Viejo several nurseries are on either side of the highway. One day, it's estimated 25,000 homes will be here, not to mention the south end of SR-241, the toll expressway that eventually connects to the dreaded SR-91 freeway.

**J**ust before reaching Interstate 5, in the midst of the usual master-planned Orange County residential area, are the Para Adobe and Harrison House.

The county reports that the adobe is believed to be to have

**Stream flows through campground.**

**Even in fog, San Juan Creek gorge is picturesque.**

been owned by early resident Miguel Para and may have served as barracks for the vaqueros from the nearby mission.

Next door, the 1905 Harrison House was once farmer John Harrison's home. The home has been restored by the city and is headquarters for the Capistrano Indian Council.

After a challenging drive, my reward was dinner at the Walnut Grove Restaurant, a San Juan Capistrano landmark since 1946. When I was a kid, we'd always stop at the Walnut Grove on the way back from Disneyland or visiting relatives in the Los Angeles area.

Still owned by the Newhart family, both the atmosphere and the food are 1950s-vintage, with pork chops, liver and onions, and meat loaf still made the old-fashioned way. Don't forget a slice of pecan

**Road is narrow and twisting.**

**Highway twists through countryside on its way to San Juan Capistrano.**

pie for dessert.

If you still have any energy left, downtown San Juan Capistrano and Mission San Juan Capistrano are within walking distance of the Walnut Grove.

Ortega Highway can be a scary drive, but it's well worth experiencing. The rural sides of Riverside and Orange counties are getting more difficult to find, but it's all here when you're ridin' on the 74.

### For More Information

- **The Diamond**, home of the Lake Elsinore Storm, *www.storm baseball.com*. Minor league baseball in cute, retro ballpark.

- **Lake Elsinore Recreation Area,** campground, boat launch, 32040 Riverside Drive, (909) 471-1212, reservations (800) 416-6992.

- **Lake Elsinore Information**, *www.pe.net/~reimbold/else.htm*. Web site looking at the funny side of the city.

- **City of Lake Elsinore**, official web site, *www.lake-elsinore.org*

- **Lookout Roadhouse**, 32107 Ortega Highway, Lake Elsinore, (909) 678-9010, *www.lookoutroadhouse.com*. Restaurant at the top of Ortega Highway grade.

- **Cleveland National Forest**, Trabuco Ranger District, 1147 East Sixth Street, Corona, (909) 736-1811, *www.fs.fed.us/r5/cleveland*. Northern end of forest has visitors' center at top of grade.

- **Ronald W. Caspers Wilderness Park**, 33401 Ortega Highway, San

Juan Capistrano, (949) 728-0235 , *www.ocparks.com/caspers*. Large open space park with camping and other activities.

- **Harrison House, Para Adobe**, 27832 Ortega Highway. Historic structures are adjacent along Ortega Highway just before Interstate 5 interchange.

- **Walnut Grove Restaurant**, 26871 Ortega Highway, San Juan Capistrano, (949) 493-1661, *www.sanjuancapistrano.net/dining/walnutgrove/index.html*. Vintage restaurant with great food and a bakery.

**Para Adobe dates to earliest Spanish settlement.**

# Index

# SUNBELT PUBLICATIONS

## "Adventures in the Natural History and Cultural Heritage of the Californias"

### *Series Editor — Lowell Lindsay*

## Southern California Series

| | |
|---|---|
| *Abracadabra: Mexican Toys* | Aceves |
| *Geology Terms in English and Spanish* | Aurand |
| *Portrait of Paloma: A Novel* | Crosby |
| *Orange County: A Photographic Collection* | Hemphill |
| *Mexican Slang Plus Graffiti* | Jones-Reid |
| *California's El Camino Real and Its Historic Bells* | Kurillo |
| *Spanish Lingo for the Savvy Gringo* | Reid |
| *Mission Memoirs: Reflections on California's Past* | Ruscin |
| *Warbird Watcher's Guide to the Southern California Skies* | Smith |
| *Campgrounds of Santa Barbara and Ventura Counties* | Tyler |
| *Campgrounds of Los Angeles and Orange Counties* | Tyler |
| *Jackpot Trail: Indian Gaming in Southern California* | Valley |

## California Desert Series

| | |
|---|---|
| *Gateway to Alta California* | Crosby |
| *Anza-Borrego A to Z: People, Places, and Things* | D. Lindsay |
| *The Anza-Borrego Desert Region* (Wilderness Press) | L. and D. Lindsay |
| *Geology of the Imperial/Mexicali Valleys* (SDAG 1998) | L. Lindsay, ed. |
| *Palm Springs Oasis: A Photographic Essay* | Lawson |
| *Desert Lore of Southern California*, 2ND edition | Pepper |
| *Peaks, Palms, and Picnics: Journeys in Coachella Valley* | Pyle |
| *Geology of Anza-Borrego: Edge of Creation* | Remeika, Lindsay |
| *Paleontology of Anza-Borrego* (SDAG 1995) | Remeika, Sturz, eds. |
| *California Desert Miracle: Parks and Wilderness* | Wheat |

## Baja California Series

| | |
|---|---|
| *The Other Side: Journeys in Baja California* | Botello |
| *Cave Paintings of Baja California*, Revised edition | Crosby |
| *Backroad Baja: The Central Region* | Higginbotham |
| *Lost Cabos: The Way it Was* (Lost Cabos Press) | Jackson |
| *Journey with a Baja Burro* | Mackintosh |
| *Houses of Los Cabos* (Amaroma) | Martinez, ed. |
| *Houses by the Sea* (Amaroma) | Martinez, ed. |
| *Mexicoland: Stories from Todos Santos* (Barking Dog Books) | Mercer |
| *Baja Legends: Historic Characters, Events, Locations* | Niemann |
| *Loreto, Baja California: First Capital* (Tio Press) | O'Neil |
| *Baja Outpost: The Guestbook from Patchen's Cabin* | Patchen |
| *Sea of Cortez Review* | Redmond |

## San Diego Series

# www.sunbeltbooks.com

## Sunbelt Publications

Incorporated in 1988 with roots in publishing since 1973, Sunbelt produces and distributes publications about "Adventures in Natural History and Cultural Heritage." These include natural science and outdoor guidebooks, regional histories and reference books, multi-language pictorials, and stories that celebrate the land and its people.

Our publishing program focuses on the Californias which are today three states in two nations sharing one Pacific shore. Somewhere in the borderland between reality and imagination, a Spanish novelist called adventurers to this region five centuries ago: "Know ye that California lies on the right hand of the Indies, very near to the terrestrial paradise."

Sunbelt books help to discover and conserve the natural and historical heritage of unique regions on the frontiers of adventure and learning. Our books guide readers into distinctive communities and special places, both natural and man-made.

*"In the end, we will conserve only what we love,
we will love only what we understand,
we will understand only what we are taught."*

— Bouba Dioum, Senegalese conservationist